The Best
Short Hikes
in the
Great
Smoky
Mountains

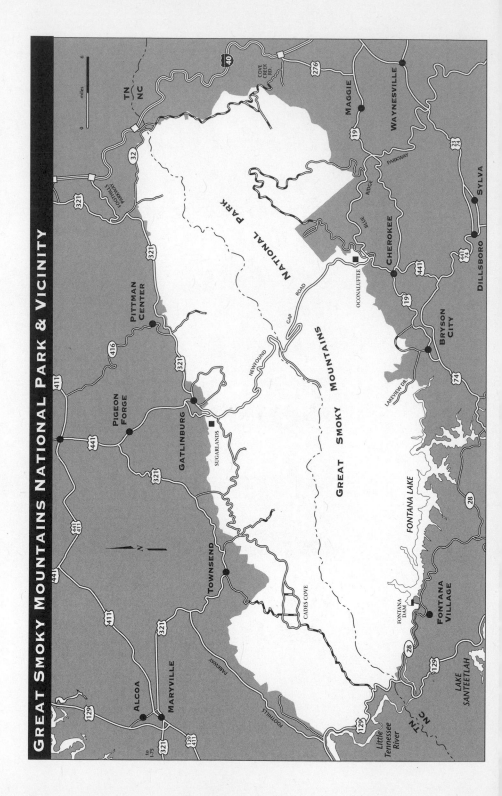

GREAT SMOKY MOUNTAINS NATIONAL PARK & VICINITY

The Best Short Hikes in the Great Smoky Mountains

Kenneth Wise and James Andrews

The University of Tennessee Press / Knoxville

Copyright © 1997 by The University of Tennessee Press/ Knoxville. All Rights Reserved. Manufactured in the United States of America. First Edition.

Frontispiece. The Great Smoky Mountains National Park.

The paper in this book meets the minimum requirements of the American National Standard for Permanence of Paper for Printed Library Materials. ∞ The binding materials have been chosen for strength and durability.

♻ Printed on recycled paper.

Map on page ii printed courtesy of the University of Tennessee Cartography Laboratory. All other maps are printed courtesy of Bill Nelson.

Library of Congress Cataloging-in-Publication Data

Wise, Kenneth, 1950–
    The best short hikes in the Great Smoky Mountains / Kenneth Wise and James Andrews.
    p. cm.
    ISBN 0-87049-973-4 (pbk. : alk. paper)
    1. Hiking—Great Smoky Mountains (N.C. and Tenn.)—Guidebooks. 2. Great Smoky Mountains (N.C. and Tenn.)—Guidebooks. I. Andrews, James, 1945– . II. Title.
GV199.42.G73W54 1997
796.5'1'0976889—dc21   96-45801
                                                CIP

Contents

Illustrations

FIGURES

MAPS

Introduction

The reason for the seemingly presumptuous title of this book is that in the Great Smoky Mountains National Park, there are well over one hundred trails tracing eight hundred miles of mountain terrain. For the hiker who is unfamiliar with the Park and has only a day or two to spend in these mountains, this book offers a selection of the trails generally accepted as the best one-day hikes in the Smokies.

Certainly no trail is intrinsically better than another, and hiking experiences cannot be critically compared on a qualitative basis; nevertheless, some trails in the Smokies enter the more majestic regions of the mountains, some pass more of the notable Smoky Mountain landmarks, and some afford spectacular vantage points that are unmatched by other trails.

On this basis, we have provided descriptions of twenty-two trails that we feel showcase the Great Smoky Mountains. These descriptions are divided into two sections: thirteen trails that we consider to be *Short Hikes,* capable of being completed within a half day, and the remaining nine, *Day Hikes,* which we estimate will take the average hiker the better part of a day to complete. Fourteen of the trails are on the Tennessee side of the mountain, six are on the North Carolina side, and two follow the stateline divide. These twenty-two trails include the prominent overlooks at Mount Le Conte, Andrews Bald, Charlies Bunion, the Jump-Off, Clingmans Dome, Thunderhead Mountain, Mount Cammerer, Silers Bald, Spence Field, and Gregory Bald. Laurel Falls, Rainbow Falls, Ramsay Cascades, Abrams Falls, Grotto Falls, and Mouse Creek Falls are among the better-known waterfalls included in this selection.

This book is intended as a beginner's introduction to hiking the Great Smoky Mountains. Nevertheless, some of the hikes are more difficult than others, and care should be taken in choosing a hike suitable to the experience and abilities of individual hikers. To assist in making these choices, the distance and elevation gain is given for each trail, as well as a brief description of the trail's general conditions.

The Great Smoky Mountains National Park is a five-hundred-thousand-acre wilderness of sculpted mountains, rushing streams, and wooded valleys astride the Tennessee–North Carolina border. This wilderness affords a unique hiking environment in which visitors can experience a wide variety of outdoor adventure. The majority of visitors to the Smokies are, however, "windshield tourists" who drive through the mountains without getting out of their cars.

This is unfortunate. With just a little effort and a few hours' time, tourists can give themselves a memorable hiking experience. The large number of maintained trails offer ridgeline and streamside hikes of varying length and difficulty. They are all well marked and frequently traveled. Consequently, there is little chance that hikers will become lost or lack assistance if they should need help. So take our advice: get out of the car and see the Smokies—arguably the most beautiful mountains east of the Rockies—at closer range.

The Great Smoky Mountains are part of the Unaka Range, a subset of the Appalachian chain. Collectively they make up the tallest range of mountains east of the Mississippi with fourteen peaks over 6,000 feet. Clingmans Dome, at 6,643 feet, is the highest mountain in the Park. Its neighbor, Mount Le Conte, is considered the tallest mountain in the Smokies since its height from base to summit is over a mile, a respectable elevation change even by Rocky Mountain standards.

The Great Smoky Mountains National Park was a joint effort of conservationists, local government, and state and federal legislatures. After considerable debate, Congress passed a bill in 1926 that allowed the federal government to take possession of the Park once Tennessee and North Carolina had secured 150,000 acres. At the time that the Park movement set about acquiring land, there were over seven thousand persons living in scattered enclaves and farms tucked into the remote hollows of the Smokies. In addition, over a dozen timber companies owned large tracts of land throughout the mountains.

Congress formally authorized the Park in 1934, even though the Civilian Conservation Corps had started work on improvements several years earlier. In 1940, President Franklin Roosevelt finally dedicated the Great Smoky Mountain National Park in a ceremony at Newfound Gap.

The Cherokees were the only residents in the Smokies when white settlers first arrived in the eighteenth century. While the Cherokees ranged throughout these mountains, they made their homes primarily in villages alongside major mountain streams and rivers. A series of broken treaties and repressive legislation finally resulted in the removal of most of the remaining Cherokee population in 1838. These hapless victims were marched to Oklahoma along the infamous Trail of Tears. Most of the Cherokees who managed to stay in the area were recognized as legal citizens of North Carolina—thanks largely to the work of a unique white man, William Holland Thomas, who was accepted as a Cherokee and even became a chief (see *Confederate Colonel and Cherokee Chief* by E. Stanly Godbold Jr. and Mattie U.

Russell [University of Tennessee Press, 1990]). This area is now called the Qualla Reservation and lies along the North Carolina edge of the Park.

A hearty breed of pioneers gradually settled in areas once inhabited by the Cherokees. Those first European settlers found a paradise of dense forests, teeming with wild game, fish, berries, and honey. The sparse crops they raised augmented their pioneer diet. Eventually, however, settlements sprang up in the more hospitable regions, such as Cades Cove, Greenbrier, Cataloochee, and Sugarlands. Larger towns had to wait until the growing nation's need for lumber and building materials brought the lumber industry to the Smokies. When lumber companies left, these mountains had been stripped of much of their forests.

However, because of moderate southern temperatures and abundant rainfall, the Smokies have recovered quickly and are once again covered with vegetation and seemingly overrun with wildlife. While some species, such as elk, cougar, and bison, are gone from the Park, there are still over seventy species of mammals found here. In addition to the smaller mammals, such as squirrels, chipmunks, and groundhogs, hikers may also spot larger animals, including deer, bears, coyotes, red wolves, foxes, and, most elusive of all, bobcats.

White-tailed deer are abundant in these mountains, and, if you hike quietly, you are almost certain to see them on any extended hike. Since all hunting is prohibited in the Park, many deer have lost their fear of humans and will often remain even when they hear people approaching. This is particularly true in the Cades Cove and Cataloochee areas, where deer leave the forest cover to graze, much like cattle, in the open meadows.

Extremely lucky hikers may get to see the "top dog" in the Park, the Smoky Mountain black bear. These shy creatures will almost always leave if they hear hikers coming, so encounters are relatively rare, especially for those hiking in groups. The black bear is much smaller and less aggressive than its western cousin, the grizzly. No one should avoid the backcountry because of black bears. Bear attacks on humans are almost unheard of and really have only occurred where people have been feeding them. When not "denned up" for the winter, the black bear is an eating machine which needs to gain enough weight to see it through the winter months. Gaining weight can literally mean life or death for these magnificent creatures, and, in years where there is a late spring freeze and the acorn crop fails, bears often leave their dens early in search of food. Those that wander out of the Park are frequently killed on the surrounding highways. Berries, nuts, rodents, and just about anything else that can be digested are vital to a healthy bear population.

The only other large mammals in the Smokies are the river otter, bobcat, coyote, red wolf, fox, and wild boar. All are very shy and not likely to be encountered by hikers. The wild boar was imported from Europe and placed in a game preserve in North Carolina. The boars eventually escaped the preserve and made their way into the Smokies, where they root for food at night and do a great deal of damage to the forest floor and the roots of trees. The Park Service runs an ongoing boar eradication program, and hikers will often encounter the big rectangular wire traps used to catch boars.

Cougars once lived in the Smokies, and, while there are often alleged sightings, hard evidence suggests that they, like the eastern bison and elk, are now extinct in this range. There is an ongoing attempt to reintroduce the red wolf, but the effort may not be successful. The river otter was successfully reintroduced in the late 1980s.

The forests seem to be layered up and down the slopes. Cove hardwoods of sugar maple, basswood, silverbell, and American beech, yellow poplar, buckeye, and red maple stand in the bottomland and on the lower flanks of the mountains. Clear-cutting was employed extensively in the lower elevations; even today, an area that was stripped of its trees is recognizable by the almost uniform diameter of the second-growth trees.

Hemlock forests with an association of rhododendron and mountain laurel cover the banks of streams as they emerge from the cove hardwood forests. Since hemlock wood was of little use to the lumber companies, very large hemlocks are frequently found alongside the mountain streams in the Park. Up until the early 1990s, dogwoods were also abundant. During those years, however, an imported fungus that thrives in cool, moist regions virtually eliminated the dogwood population. Drier, sunny areas support a variety of oak trees and pines. Shaded and protected areas hold mostly birch and beech trees.

Red spruce and Fraser fir dominate the highest peaks. This association, abundant on the Canadian tundra, is unique to the Smokies in the United States. Unfortunately, the balsam woolly adelgid, an imported parasite, has killed most of the mature Fraser firs. Where these densely growing evergreens once stood, the mountain tops are now home to a sea of dead and graying tree trunks. There is some evidence that the spruce trees are dependent on the Fraser firs, and with the demise of the firs the spruce are now showing signs of stress.

The tree species once dominant in the Smokies was the American chestnut. Because it blossomed later in the spring and avoided late frosts, it was a very reliable source of food for the bear population and other animals. Earlier this century the chestnut trees were killed by an exotic fungus imported into this country around 1900. Efforts to develop a resistant variety of the American chestnut have so far proven unsuccessful.

Occasionally, a peak will be covered in either grass or shrubs rather than trees. These are known as "balds," and their origins remain a mystery. Since they are prime grazing areas, eastern bison and elk probably kept them "mowed," and, when settlers arrived from North Carolina, cattle and sheep took over the job. Today, with neither wild nor domestic animals to graze them, the balds are being slowly invaded by the surrounding forest.

Despite all the human-made problems, however, the Smokies are still quite resilient. The various blights and parasites only make room for new species to replace the old. With luck, future generations will enjoy backcountry hikes almost identical to those described in this book. The hikes we have included will take visitors to the most beautiful and readily accessible places in the Smokies, areas that are truly worth seeing over and over again.

Preparing for a Backcountry Hike

Permits

No permits are required for a day hike.

Preparation

We always take reasonable precautions, even though nothing presents a significant risk on these trails. A hiker literally has a better chance of being struck by lightning than getting attacked by a bear, bitten by a snake, or getting lost. That said, here is some information that might make your hike more pleasant:

1. Wear sturdy, stiff-soled shoes that provide good ankle support. There are loose rocks on every trail, and a good pair of hiking boots is the best way to avoid a sprained ankle.
2. If there is more than one person in your party, spread the load and make sure part of the load includes toilet paper and insect repellent.
3. Each person in the party should have a good whistle readily available while hiking. This is more effective, and less exhausting, than shouting for one another in the unlikely event that you become separated. It might also terrify and chase off an overly aggressive bear.
4. Take good food. Pack weight on a day hike is normally not a problem.
5. On a hot day, freeze your water the night before the hike in plastic soda bottles. These will help keep your picnic lunch fresh, and the ice-cold water tastes great after an hour or two of hiking.

Park Rules

1. For toilet use, walk at least one hundred feet from the trail, while glancing back to be certain of the trail's location. Be sure you are well away from a water source or campsite, and then dig a hole at least six inches deep using a shovel or the heel of your boot. Cover the hole with dirt when you are finished.
2. Bag all trash and haul it out with you.
3. Do not pick or cut flowers, berries, trees, or other foliage.
4. Do not feed the wildlife. Animals that learn to look to humans for food are doomed in the winter when there is no one around to feed them.

Precautions

There are only a few important backpacking dangers. The most life-threatening is hypothermia. Storms and sudden temperature drops can occur very quickly in these mountains. Always carry a poncho or a rain suit. If you do not have either one, take several large plastic trash bags with you. With some trash bags and a little duct tape, a resourceful hiker can make it through just about any summer storm.

Proper rain gear will keep you dry and hold in body heat. We always leave a dry change of clothing in the car, however, so that no matter what happens we do not have to drive home wearing wet clothes.

Other problems that befall hikers with some frequency are sprained ankles and twisted knees. These injuries often occur when someone slips on a rock while crossing a stream. If the stream crossing looks particularly difficult, take off your boots and wade it; it is often quicker and easier than wandering around on the bank searching for those perfectly placed rocks.

Lastly, dehydration or heat exhaustion can become a problem for hikers who do not drink enough water or take frequent rest stops. A handy way to keep cool is to wear a wet bandanna around your forehead. There are plenty of streams and springs for rewetting, and, especially on a hot summer day, a bandanna can quickly become your favorite piece of equipment. There is no substitute, however, for drinking plenty of water.

First Aid

1. Bring along a well-equipped first aid kit.
2. Snake bite is a rare event. In fact, there has never been a fatality from a snake bite in the Park. All snakes try to avoid human contact, and encounters, especially with poisonous snakes, seldom occur. As a precaution, however, carry an inexpensive snakebite kit (available in any outdoor store), and follow the included instructions in the event that someone is bitten.
3. Blisters, however, are not rare. Wear two pairs of socks, and bring plenty of mole skin (a tough adhesive padding). Stop at the first sign of irritation and put mole skin on the affected area.
4. Bee stings may be the biggest first aid problem in the park. Throw an inexpensive "bee sting stick" and some antihistamine in your pack just in case.

We always adhere to the precautions we have suggested. It gives us a secure feeling when we hike that we will be prepared for any emergency. These mountains, because of the relatively low altitude and the good condition of the trails, are very safe for hiking. The hikes in this book are an enjoyable way for visitors to get to know most of the major backcountry regions in this wonderful wilderness. By undertaking even a short hike, you can go home and tell people what you experienced while you were in the Smokies rather than merely what you saw there. In addition, planning a short hike is a great way to gain valuable experience to plan a longer visit.

Short Hikes

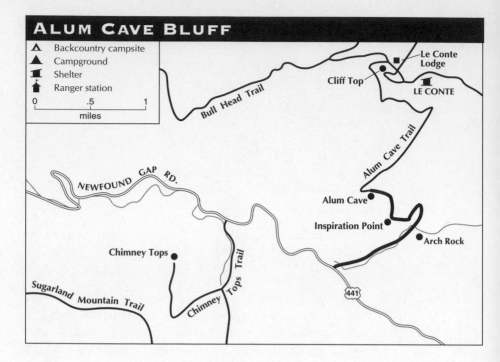

ALUM CAVE BLUFF

- △ Backcountry campsite
- ▲ Campground
- ⬛ Shelter
- ♦ Ranger station

0   .5   1
miles

Bull Head Trail

Le Conte Lodge

Cliff Top

LE CONTE

Alum Cave Trail

NEWFOUND GAP RD.

Alum Cave

Inspiration Point

Arch Rock

Chimney Tops

Chimney Tops Trail

Sugarland Mountain Trail

441

ALUM CAVE BLUFF

Distance: 4.6 miles round-trip.

Elevation gain: 1,400 feet.

Brief trail description: The trail to Alum Cave Bluff is one of the finest short excursions in the Smokies. It traverses a rugged mountain terrain that possesses a panoply of notable landmarks, scenic overlooks, and unusual geological features. The trail is fairly level along its streamside course but becomes markedly steeper as it climbs away from the stream to Alum Cave Bluff. While this trail is an ideal distance for a family outing, it may perhaps be a little too rugged for younger children.

How to get there: Drive to the Alum Cave parking area on the Newfound Gap Road (US 441) 8.6 miles southeast of the Sugarlands Visitor Center, or 4.3 miles northwest of Newfound Gap. The trail begins along the gravel path adjacent to the parking area.

0.0—Grassy Patch.

1.4—Arch Rock.

1.5—Huggins Hell.

1.8—Inspiration Point.

2.3—Alum Cave Bluff.

The Alum Cave Trail begins at the Grassy Patch, a highland clearing that once harbored a crude hunters' cabin. The cabin is long gone, and the clearing is now paved over and occupied by a parking lot.

After leaving the Grassy Patch, the Alum Cave Bluff Trail follows a pleasant streamside course through the bottoms along Alum Cave Creek. The stream is flanked by a splendid forest of hemlock and yellow birch that shades thickets of sprawling rhododendron. Along this stretch, the trail is fairly level, and several paths leading from the main trail offer access to the many pools on Alum Cave Creek.

Approximately one mile above the Grassy Patch, Alum Cave Creek is joined by its main tributary, Styx Branch. This stream was so named because of its origin deep within the vast expanse of Huggins Hell. Early settlers often referred to large rhododendron and laurel patches as "hells," and any hiker who has tried to penetrate one without the benefit of a well-maintained trail will readily agree with the name.

Near the confluence of the two streams, the trail leaves Alum Cave Creek and follows Styx Branch a half-mile. It crosses Styx Branch for the third time immediately underneath Arch Rock, a rocky rib of black slate slanting down from the mountain to the creek. Arch Rock has a tunnel-like hole slanting through it, twenty feet high at the bottom and six feet high at its upper opening. The hole is clearly not the work of erosion, for the surfaces are not smooth but jagged and broken, perhaps the result of stress fractures in the rock strata that were gradually riven apart by the action of cold and ice. Steps take the hiker up and through Arch Rock, and the trail continues beside Styx Branch, crossing it for the last time at the mouth of Huggins Hell.

According to a bit of mountain lore preserved by Paul Fink in his monograph *That's Why They Call It . . . The Names and Lore of the Great Smokies,* the name "Huggins Hell" was attributed to a certain gentleman named Huggins who "vowed he'd explore the wilderness if it took him to Hell. He was never heard from again and, popularly, was supposed to have carried out the alternative."

Two hundred yards beyond Styx Branch is the site of one of the most astounding natural disasters in the Smokies. In the early evening of June 28, 1993, a heavy thunderstorm rolled across the Tennessee Valley and plowed into the face of Mount Le Conte, releasing several inches of rain onto one spot near the summit. The water gathered quickly along the higher slopes, forming a raging torrent that was sent roaring down a narrow defile on the south face. The weight of the moisture in the humus and the scouring action of the rainwater, which could not be absorbed, combined in a devastating way to rip a raw gash down the mountainside. Huge hemlocks, nearly four feet in diameter, were clipped with such force that they were toppled upstream. The smaller vegetation and the soil cover were stripped away, leaving freshly scoured bedrock and large, heavy boulders scattered throughout the stream bed.

The wave of this highland flood was estimated to have been twenty feet high. It struck quickly, causing its destruction in less than five minutes. In the process, a seam of highly acidic Anakeesta rock was left exposed, and the distinct smell of sulfur is evidence that its caustic effluent was leaching out. This leaching may continue for several decades. Farther up the trail, at Alum Cave Bluff, is a graphic example of the long-term effects of this sulfuric leaching onto the mountain.

A half-mile above Arch Rock, at the corner of a sharp right turn in the trail, is Inspiration Point, the first real opportunity for a panoramic view of the neighborhood. To the southeast is Anakeesta Ridge, stretching to its terminus near the Grassy Patch. Immediately to the west are two outliers, Little Duckhawk Ridge and Big Duckhawk Ridge, one behind the other, which project southward from the base of Alum Cave. Alum Cave itself is not quite visible from this vantage point as it is tucked in a little too far against the ridge. Just beneath its highest peak, Little Duckhawk Ridge sports an impressive hole in its side, as though it had been shot through with a cannon ball. Only the peaks of Big Duckhawk Ridge can be seen above its nearer twin. Both, however, are accessible by separate manways that leave the main trail a few hundred yards above Alum Cave.

Indian lore indicates that Alum Cave was first sighted by the famous Cherokee Chief Yanugunski while he was tracking a bear to its den. Alum Cave, however, is not really a cave, but a massive ledge composed of black slate that juts straight out from the mountain face high above the trail. The slate contains traces of iron sulfide, which, when moistened by rainwater trickling through the crevices in the rock, forms a weak solution of sulfuric acid. The acid decomposes the slate, causing the deep layer of dust that covers the floor of the cave.

The name "Alum Cave" is derived from the encrustation of alum along the back walls of the cave. Although the mineral deposits found here are of insufficient quan-

Alum Cave Bluff. Courtesy of Jim Thompson.

tity to be of any commercial value, the cave has occasionally been mined for alum, saltpeter, copperas, and magnesia. In the 1830s a group from Oconaluftee formed the Epsom Salts Manufacturing Company to exploit these deposits, and it is claimed, spuriously perhaps, that saltpeter mined from the cave during the Civil War was of great value to the Confederacy. 🚶🚶

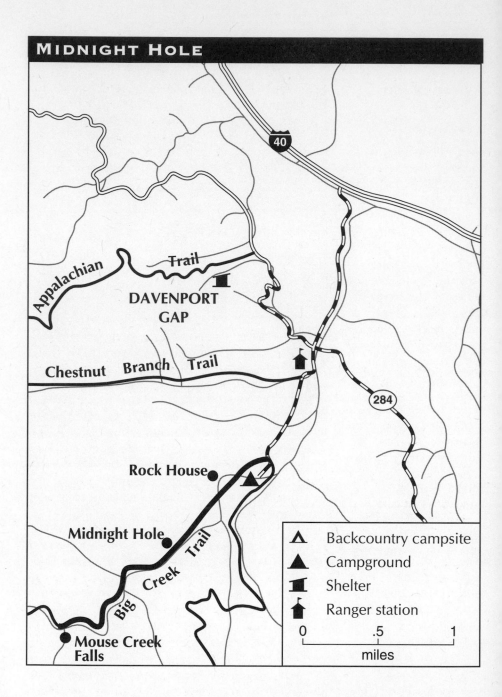

Appalachian Trail

DAVENPORT GAP

Chestnut Branch Trail

40

284

Rock House

Midnight Hole

Big Creek Trail

Mouse Creek Falls

△	Backcountry campsite
▲	Campground
⌶	Shelter
⌂	Ranger station

0   .5   1

miles

Distance: 4.0 miles round-trip.

Elevation gain: 200 feet.

Brief trail description: Midnight Hole, a remarkable pool at the foot of a short waterfall on Big Creek, affords an excellent destination for a family outing in the Smokies. The trail to Midnight Hole is a wide, easy, streamside excursion and offers a variety of unusual mountain scenes. The trail follows the keel of a deep gulf bounded on the north by the stateline divide, on the south by Mount Sterling Ridge, and enclosed on its upper end by Balsam Mountain. The Big Creek Basin, although easily accessed, lies in one of the more remote sectors of the Park and is unlikely to be crowded with hikers.

How to get there: On I-40 drive 60 miles east from Knoxville or 50 miles west from Asheville to the Waterville exit. Cross the Pigeon River and follow the road upstream to the power plant of the Carolina Power and Light Company. At the power plant, the road turns and proceeds 2 miles to an intersection with old NC

284 at the Mount Sterling community. Pass through the intersection. The Big Creek ranger station is 0.2 mile along the road. About 0.7 mile beyond the ranger station the Big Creek Trail begins on the right. The trail to Midnight Hole follows the Big Creek Trail. Parking is available just below the trailhead, near the picnic area.

0.0—Big Creek Road (parking area).

1.0—Rock House.

1.4—Midnight Hole.

2.0—Mouse Creek Falls.

The trail to Midnight Hole begins at the lower end of an elongated basin that harbors the course of Big Creek. Initially the trail charts a course away from the stream, along the upper edge of the basin floor. Within the first few hundred yards the stream swings abruptly across the basin to press the trail against the adjacent slope. The stream shifts quickly back to its original position, then back again to the trail as both the stream and trail are marshaled into the pinched gorge that forms the keel of the big basin. Beyond this point, the trail rarely strays more than a few yards from Big Creek.

The steadfast ruggedness of the Big Creek basin is nowhere better exemplified than at the Rock House, a jumble of massive boulders scattered along the slope one mile above the trailhead. A steep path climbs two hundred feet above the trail to several huge blocks of stone, one of which is notched deeply at its corner, forming a roomy alcove. Its vertical walls join at a precisely perpendicular angle and the remarkably flat, thirty-foot high ceiling forms a protective overhang sheltering the interior. Early settlers inhabited the Rock House temporarily while building more permanent homes along Big Creek.

The trail continues another easy half-mile before coming to Midnight Hole, an attractive pool spanning the width of Big Creek. The pool is twelve feet deep at

Midnight Hole on Big Creek. Courtesy of Lou A. Murray.

the back and slopes gradually fifty feet downstream to a depth of one foot. Its emerald green water is so clear that each pebble on the pool's bottom is clearly visible. Along the upper side, two large boulders form a low cliff. The stream is squeezed through a gap between the boulders, then fans out in a translucent sheet of water plunging ten feet into the pool. Midnight Hole is the best known of several clear pools spaced irregularly along Big Creek, places where the slow-moving stream collects before easing off and resuming its journey out of the mountains.

Hikers with extra time may wish to venture another easy half-mile uptrail to Mouse Creek Falls. Here Mouse Creek makes a splashy entry into Big Creek, cascading fifty feet down the face of a rocky cliff. Several individual streamlets descend irregularly to an abandoned logging road where they gather momentarily before dropping a final ten feet to Big Creek. A short path leads up to a bench on the edge of Big Creek directly opposite where Mouse Creek Falls joins the parent stream. 🚶

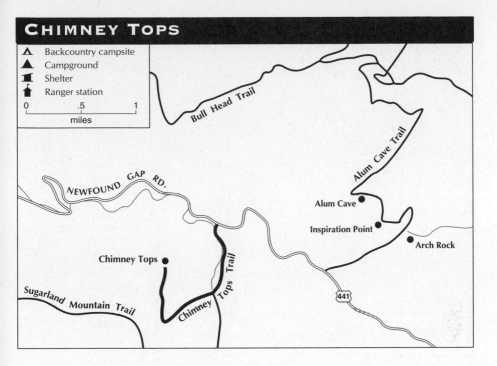

CHIMNEY TOPS

- △ Backcountry campsite
- ▲ Campground
- ▣ Shelter
- ⬚ Ranger station

0   .5   1
miles

Bull Head Trail

Alum Cave Trail

NEWFOUND GAP RD.

Alum Cave ●

Inspiration Point ●

Arch Rock ●

Chimney Tops ●

Chimney Tops Trail

Sugarland Mountain Trail

441

Distance: 4.0 miles round-trip.

Elevation gain: 1,400 feet.

Brief trail description: The trail to the Chimney Tops is short but steep and leads to one of the finest vantage points for panoramic viewing anywhere in the Smokies. Its course is moderately level for the first mile, then enters a rather stiff 600-yard climb. The final ascent to the top requires a brief hand-over-hand scramble up a steeply pitched, rocky face. The scramble is not particularly dangerous but may be difficult for small children.

How to get there: Drive on the Newfound Gap Road (US 441) 6.7 miles southeast of the Sugarlands Visitor Center or 6.2 miles northwest of Newfound Gap to the Chimney Tops parking area. The Chimney Tops Trail begins just beyond the low rock wall bordering the parking area.

0.0—Newfound Gap Road (parking area).

0.9—Beech Flats. Road Prong Trail leads left.

2.0—Chimney Tops.

The Chimney Tops are perhaps the most conspicuous and readily identifiable landmarks in the Smokies. Presiding over a deep, steep-sided defile that separates the razor-edge Sugarland Mountain from Mount Le Conte and Huggins Hell, the Chimney Tops loom like shattered spires of a ruined cathedral long since abandoned to the forces of time. Buttressed by a rugged spur that extends from the wall of Sugarland Mountain, they project like ramparts high over the valley of the West Prong of the Little Pigeon River.

The Cherokee moniker for the Chimney Tops was Duniskwalguni, meaning "forked antlers." The name obviously refers to their understanding of the mountain as being two peaks emanating from a common base. The modern designation, "Chimney Tops," or simply "the Chimneys," was bequeathed to the peaks by the pioneering white mountaineers who, in accordance with their custom, generally referred to any stack formation of rock extending above the surrounding terrain as a "chimney." The fact that the taller spire has a hole down its center merely serves to reinforce and popularize the name.

The Chimney Tops Trail begins along the Newfound Gap Road near the confluence of Walker Camp Prong and Road Prong, which forms the West Prong of the Little Pigeon River. The trail descends quickly to a sturdy bridge over Walker Camp Prong. A few yards beyond, a similar bridge spans Road Prong.

Immediately beyond the second bridge, the trail turns left and enters a streamside course along Road Prong, a brawling torrent that plunges over boulders and ledges. The precursor to this section of the trail is an ancient Cherokee trace that crossed the mountain at Indian Gap and descended to the Great Indian War Path leading out of Tennessee. During the Civil War, this Indian trail was converted into a road by a force of six hundred Cherokees under the direction of Colonel "Little Will" Thomas, for use by the warring armies of the Union and Confederacy. Even with these improvements, the condition of the road was still such that the soldiers had to dismount the cannon from their carriages and drag them by hand over the boulder-strewn road. After the war the Thomas Road was used sparingly by farmers hauling produce and driving cattle from North Carolina to the markets in the Tennessee Valley.

One mile into the hike, the trail enters Beech Flats, a former settlement clearing now invaded by a thin copse of hemlock and birch with an understory of scrawny beech. Early visitors to Beech Flats recall that the upper and lower ends of the flat were blocked by pole livestock fences.

In Beech Flats the Chimney Tops Trail intersects the lower terminus of the Road Prong Trail. Here the Chimney Tops Trail turns right, leaving the Road Prong Trail to follow along the old Thomas Road to Indian Gap.

On leaving Beech Flats, the Chimney Tops Trail climbs into a deep ravine that furrows the steep north slope of Sugarland Mountain. An enormous yellow buckeye marks the end of a steep, six-hundred-yard grind up the ravine and the first of two switchbacks that position the trail high enough up Sugarland Mountain to mount the spur leading to the Chimneys. Above the switchbacks, the trail traces a rough berm cut into the rocky slope of Sugarland Mountain. About two hundred yards from trail's end, the berm grades into the spur connecting the Chimneys with

The Chimney Tops. Courtesy of Jim Thompson.

Sugarland Mountain. The trail then approaches the Chimneys at the base of the higher spire.

The final ascent of the Chimneys is a rugged hand-over-hand scramble up the rocky side of the taller spire. Its top is barren, worn by generations of hikers coming here to experience the exhilaration of standing perilously close to a precarious edge. The shorter spire is linked to the taller by a hideously thin spur, one of the few, true knife-edges in the Smokies. The climb between the peaks is fraught with slithery surfaces and narrow ledges.

From the Chimneys, the most noticeable landmark is Mount Le Conte, looming immediately above the valley of the West Prong. Mount Le Conte is an outlier, standing five miles apart from the main Smoky Mountain divide, but connected to it by the Boulevard, a high tortuous ridge that can be seen leading east from Le Conte to Mount Kephart. Immediately to the east is Mount Mingus, a promontory at the end of Mingus Lead.

The grander views are perhaps those to the west where receding ranges of mountain are defined by subtle gradations in color rather than any fixed landmarks or boundaries. Far below, the immense forested valley of the Sugarlands sweeps down from the western flank of Mount Le Conte. At the bottom of the valley, automobiles can be seen passing along the Newfound Gap Road as it winds through the rugged mountain contours.

The summit of the Chimney Tops is not spacious, but it is sufficient to accommodate a small group of picnickers. Crags, ramparts, and boulders around the summit provide convenient perches on which to sit back, relax, and enjoy the magnificent scenery. 🚶🚶

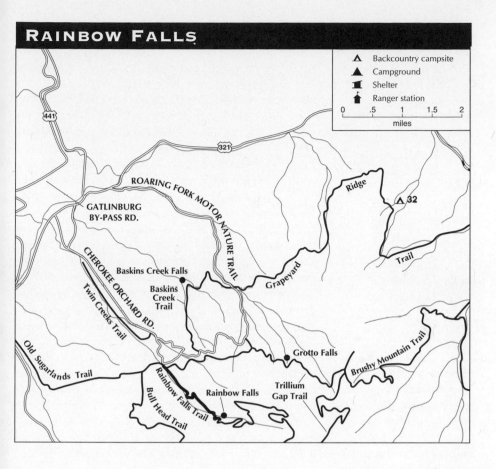

RAINBOW FALLS

Legend:
- ⚠ Backcountry campsite
- ▲ Campground
- ▬ Shelter
- ⚑ Ranger station

0 .5 1 1.5 2
miles

441

321

ROARING FORK MOTOR NATURE TRAIL

GATLINBURG BY-PASS RD.

CHEROKEE ORCHARD RD.

Ridge

△ 32

Baskins Creek Falls

Baskins Creek Trail

Twin Creeks Trail

Grapeyard

Trail

Old Sugarlands Trail

Grotto Falls

Brushy Mountain Trail

Rainbow Falls Trail

Rainbow Falls

Trillium Gap Trail

Bull Head Trail

RAINBOW FALLS

Distance: 5.6 miles round-trip.

Elevation gain: 1,750 feet.

Brief trail description: The trail to Rainbow Falls is one of the more difficult of the shorter trails. Its grade is rarely steep and rough. The trail alternates between dry-ridge hardwoods and deep hemlock forest, and often follows a streamside course. It terminates at Rainbow Falls, the highest waterfall in the Smokies.

How to get there: Follow Airport Road 1.0 mile out of Gatlinburg into the Park. At the Park boundary the road continues, but the name changes to Cherokee Orchard Road. About 3.4 miles after entering the Park, the road becomes one-way. Just above this juncture is the Rainbow Falls parking area to the right of the road. The trail begins on the upper corner of the parking area.

0.0—Cherokee Orchard Road.

2.8—Rainbow Falls.

The earliest trail to Rainbow Falls was a fisherman's trace that followed up the east side of Le Conte Creek. Le Conte Creek was then known as Mill Creek, so called because of the dozen or so grist mills that operated along the stream. The grist mills served the farming community that subsisted along the bottomlands of lower Mill Creek, an area known generally as Cherokee Orchard.

The present trail to Rainbow Falls begins in the upper end of Cherokee Orchard along Le Conte Creek, twisting and turning its way through a field of boulders scattered widely across the gently sloping terrain. Hemlocks and a variety of cove hardwoods shade a thin understory of ferns, casting an aura of primeval spaciousness over the rugged wilderness. Le Conte Creek, one of the more charming in the Smokies, reflects the somber browns and greens of an ancient and undisturbed forest. The trail generally follows the course of Le Conte Creek, affording several nice views down into the stream's gorge.

One mile above Cherokee Orchard the trail swings away from the stream onto an exposed finger ridge of pines and dry-ridge hardwoods. The trail soon returns to the stream, crossing it on a footlog before beginning a series of climbing switchbacks through the closed gloom of a deep hemlock stand.

At the second stream crossing, a high fortress-like cliff is faintly visible upstream through the over-reaching branches of the trees, set back in a high amphitheater. The cliff is sequestered in thickets of rhododendron and surrounded by a hemlock forest that filters the sunlight, producing an eerie twilight. Its massive edifice is crowned by a huge protruding ledge over which descends Rainbow Falls.

Rainbow Falls comes into complete view at the upper footlog where the trail crosses Le Conte Creek for the third time. A closer view is afforded by scrambling

Rainbow Falls. Courtesy of Great Smoky Mountains National Park.

over the rocks and approaching the falls along the lower ledge. The area around the falls is usually wet and can be very slick.

At this point Le Conte Creek is a rather small stream, and its weak flow disperses into a heavy mist before striking the flat, solid surface eighty-three feet below. An appropriate angle of sunlight reflecting off the descending mist casts a rainbow across the face of the cliff. One of the best times to visit Rainbow Falls is during the coldest part of winter. If the air is sufficiently cold, mist from the falls freezes as it descends, forming a tremendous, jagged pinnacle of ice reaching to the brink of the falls. The icy blue-whiteness of the pinnacle against the pale, reflected light of the rocky amphitheater composes an unusual panorama. 🏃

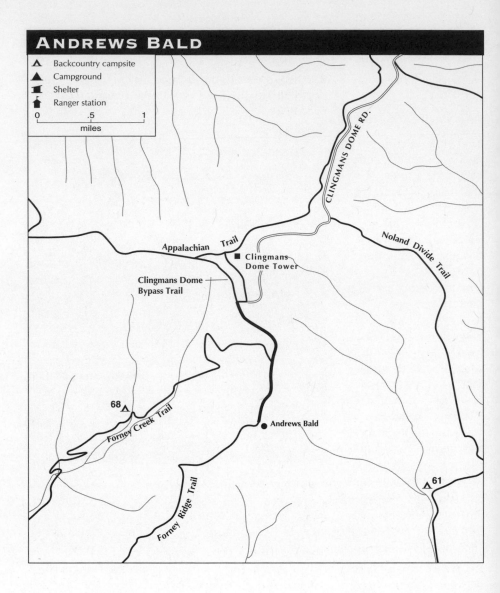

ANDREWS BALD

Backcountry campsite
Campground
Shelter
Ranger station

0   .5   1
miles

CLINGMANS DOME RD.

Appalachian   Trail

Clingmans
Dome Tower

Noland Divide Trail

Clingmans Dome
Bypass Trail

68△

Forney Creek Trail

● Andrews Bald

△61

Forney Ridge Trail

Distance: 3.6 miles round-trip.

Elevation loss: 500 feet.

Brief Trail description: Andrews Bald, the highest bald in the Smokies, is an expansive, pitched meadow straddling the spine of Forney Ridge about two miles below Clingmans Dome. The trail to Andrews Bald traces the upper end of the Forney Ridge Trail beginning at the far end of the Clingmans Dome Road parking area just where the paved path to the Clingmans Dome Tower leaves the road. The trail is moderately steep and its course rocky and uneven. On a clear day, the bald affords an exceptional vantage point for surveying unending layers of mountains receding into western North Carolina.

How to get there: From the Sugarlands Visitor Center, drive southeast on US 441 12.9 miles to Newfound Gap, or, from the Oconaluftee Visitor Center, 15.9 miles northwest. At Newfound Gap, turn south onto the Clingmans Dome Road and drive 7.0 miles to its end. The trail to Andrews

Bald begins on the Forney Ridge Trail near where the paved track to the Clingmans Dome Tower leaves the parking area.

0.0—Clingmans Dome Road (parking area).

0.2—Clingmans Dome Bypass Trail leads right.

1.1—Forney Creek Trail leads right.

1.8—Andrews Bald.

 On leaving the Clingmans Dome parking area, the trail to Andrews Bald descends a steep 150 yards through a jumble of rocks to an intersection with the lower terminus of the Clingmans Dome Bypass Trail. At this juncture, the trail turns sharply left and descends moderately along a well-worn rocky berm. In places the trail may be saturated with water gushing from hidden outlets nestled along the berm's upper edge.

The trail continues descending through a thin spruce-fir forest mixed generously with mountain ash, until leveling out into a long narrow swag about halfway between Clingmans Dome Road and Andrews Bald. The mountain ash, often regarded as the most boreal of the deciduous trees in the Smokies, is plentiful along this stretch of trail and strikingly attractive in late summer and early fall when bearing its vivid, red-orange clusters of fruit.

The lowest point in the swag is marked by an intersection with the upper terminus of the Forney Creek Trail on the right. From this juncture the approach to Andrews Bald is a gently sloped, one-mile climb.

The trail enters Andrews Bald from its upper end. On a clear day the view from the bald is astonishing. Along its east edge lies a vast gulf, boldly defined by the Noland Divide, solid, forested with subtle gradations in color. To the west is Welch Ridge, punctuated at its lower end by a rounded knoll known as High Rocks. In the great vale below, Fontana Lake appears as a sleeping dragon curled in among the lower ridges of the

Andrews Bald. Courtesy of Great Smoky Mountains National Park.

Smokies and the Nantahalas. And beyond this, layers upon layers of mountains extend far beyond where the horizon dissolves into the blue sky.

The origin of the name "Andrews Bald" is not clear. According to one tradition, Andrews is a corruption of "Anders," the family name of herders who once used the bald as an upland pasture for their browsing stock. According to another, it was named for Andreas Thompson, a pioneering settler who built a cabin and enlarged the bald in 1852 for his cattle. In either case, only the corrupted namesake has survived and is now universally adopted in Smoky Mountain literature.

The Anders and other herder families occupied a cabin that stood along the original, lower fringe of the bald on a site now several yards into the forest. After the grazing ceased, the forest reclaimed some of the turf. Today Andrews Bald is occupied by pockets of irregularly spaced flame azalea and rhododendron which in late spring offer dazzling floral displays similar to the famed exhibitions on Gregory Bald.

One of the absorbing mysteries of the Great Smoky Mountains is the origin of the balds. Are they a natural phenomenon or human-made? Several theories have been advanced supporting both sides of this issue, but one of the more interesting is the speculation that the seam between the balsam zone and the deciduous hardwoods represents a near timber-line condition. Along this seam there is a constant imbalance due to weather changes. Somewhere in this area the weather becomes too warm for the balsams and, similarly, too cold or otherwise unfavorable for the spread of hardwoods. Wherever species of the balsam zone or the hardwoods occupy space in the balds, they do so gingerly and without much conviction. Any long-term shift in weather conditions would tend to strike down or inhibit the growth of the species most susceptible to that particular fluctuation. Thus there is never really any occupation by either the balsams or hardwoods, but only a patrol action which could quickly be driven back by a change in weather. This suggests that the balds are a natural occurrence in this in-between zone where conditions are unfavorable for either species.

The wide open spaces on Andrews Bald are popular with hikers who enjoy being comfortably ensconced on the thick mountain grass with a picnic lunch. The proximity of the deep forests, the magnificent views of the receding layers of mountains, and the palpable sense of being in a high place make Andrews Bald a place unmatched by any other in the Smokies. 🚶

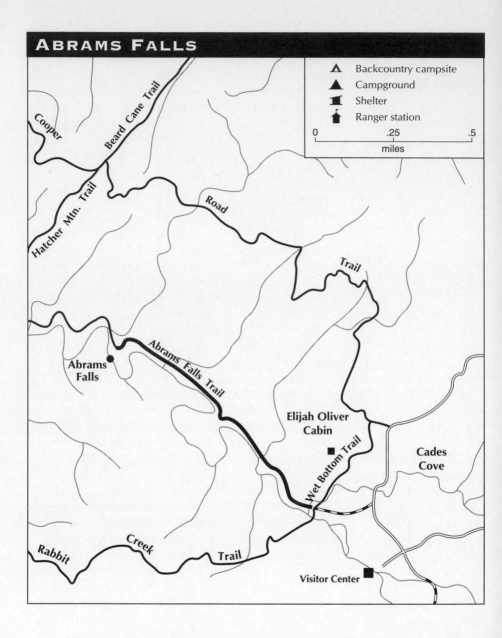

ABRAMS FALLS

Legend:
- △ Backcountry campsite
- ▲ Campground
- ▣ Shelter
- ⌂ Ranger station

0   .25   .5
miles

Cooper

Beard Cane Trail

Hatcher Mtn. Trail

Road

Trail

Abrams Falls

Abrams Falls Trail

Elijah Oliver Cabin

Wet Bottom Trail

Cades Cove

Rabbit Creek Trail

Visitor Center

ABRAMS FALLS

Distance: 5.0 miles round-trip.

Elevation loss: 300 feet.

Brief trail description: The Abrams Falls Trail is an easy well-graded course that leads to one of the largest waterfalls in the Smokies. Because of its proximity to Cades Cove, this trail is always one of the most popular in the Park.

How to get there: Enter the Park at Townsend, Tennessee, and drive 1.0 mile to the Townsend Wye where the Little River Road intersects the Laurel Creek Road. Or, from the Sugarlands Visitor Center, drive west on the Little River Road 18.8 miles to the Wye. Turn onto Laurel Creek Road and drive 7.0 miles to Cades Cove, then along the Cades Cove Loop Road 4.6 miles to a quarter-mile gravel access leading to the Abrams Falls Trail. The trail begins at the parking area at the end of the gravel road.

0.0—Wooden bridge over Abrams Creek. Connection leads right 0.5 mile to the Elijah Oliver Place.

1.0—Arbutus Ridge viewpoint over Big Horseshoe.

2.5—Path leads left 50 yards to Abrams Falls.

The trail to Abrams Falls begins at the extreme western end of Cades Cove, a remarkably flat limestone basin four miles long and one mile wide, and completely surrounded by high mountains. Thunderhead Mountain and the stateline divide define its south boundary and Rich Mountain the north. The east end abuts Bote Mountain, and the west is blocked by Hatcher and Hannah Mountains.

The cove is drained by Abrams Creek, the largest stream whose course lies entirely within the Park. The Cades Cove Loop Road, undoubtedly the most popular motor trail in the Park, circles the perimeter of the cove and passes several restored homesites and other artifacts of nineteenth-century Appalachia.

Of particular interest are the John Oliver Cabin, the oldest log building in the cove, and Cables Mill, a remnant of the cove's industrial period. The loop road also passes cabins, barns, farms, churches, and cemeteries that were an integral part of the thriving settlement that once stood on this fertile bottomland.

The large meadows which make up the floor of the cove are primarily used to graze cattle. Often, however, when touring the cove we see deer grazing on the rich meadow grasses. As a matter of fact, a couple of years ago, this pastoral mountain meadow was the scene of a dark episode in the history of Smoky Mountain wildlife.

Two hunters from Florida, outfitted with high-powered rifles, silencers, and night scopes slithered into the Park after dark and poached two magnificent buck deer. Pictures of these deer, named "Streamer" and "Tims Ten" by Forest Service ranger and wildlife photographer Bill Lea, had been on the covers of numerous outdoor magazines. Luckily these two "sportsmen" were arrested by Park Service Rangers and spent over two years in a federal penitentiary for their crimes.

Poaching, especially of black bears, is a very serious problem in the Park. The bears gall bladders are prized in oriental herbal medicine for their perceived ability to cure impotence. Unfortunately, the Park is large and the dedicated ranger staff is seriously underfunded. So, if you enjoy your time in these lush mountains, let your representative and your senators know that you support funding for the national parks. We once had a congressman tell us that if he gets fifty letters on a subject he considers it a groundswell. So take the time to write. We enjoy seeing bears when we go into the Smoky Mountains and want our grandchildren to see them as well.

Eighteen streams drain the slopes of the Cades Cove basin into Abrams Creek as it courses westward through the center of the cove. The creek exits Cades Cove through an aperture on the lower end, then winds its way through a narrow gorge to its mouth at Chilhowee Lake, near the southwest corner of the Park.

The name "Abrams" is a truncation of "Abraham," erstwhile chief of the Cherokees who led the last Indian attacks on Watauga settlement. Chief Abram's camp, Chilhowee Village, was on the Little Tennessee near the mouth of the stream now known as Abrams Creek.

The trail to the falls begins where Abrams Creek leaves the openness of Cades Cove and begins winding its way through the mountains. The trail immediately crosses the stream on a sturdy wooden bridge, then turns left to follow Abrams Creek downstream. At the end of the bridge, another trail leads right to the Elijah Oliver place about a half-mile up the cove.

For its first mile the trail is a pleasant level course along the wide creek. Occasionally one may spot a fisherman or two angling for the elusive rainbow trout that thrive in this cold stream. The rainbow trout were introduced into Abrams Creek by John Oliver, a descendent of Elijah Oliver. Unfortunately the rainbow trout and the brown trout, which were introduced later, are more aggressive than the native brook trout and have forced the "brookies" into the higher-elevation streams. The brook trout are a threatened species in the Smokies, and it is illegal to fish for them or to retain them if they are taken accidentally.

The first substantial rise in the trail occurs at Arbutus Ridge where the trail leaves the stream and climbs up into a gap in the ridge from where Abrams Creek can be seen two hundred feet below as it enters the Big Horseshoe. At the Big Horseshoe, the stream traces a wide circle, a mile in circumference, before returning almost to the point where it started. The lower end of the ridge forms a narrow neck separating the ends of the loop.

On descending Arbutus Ridge, the trail rejoins the stream. It rises occasionally to clear another low ridge or two before descending to the mouth of Wilson Creek. Here a short side trail leads left to Abrams Falls.

At the falls, the slow-paced Abrams Creek is funneled into a chute along the far side, transforming the stream into a raging torrent plunging over a ledge and into one of the largest natural pools in the Smokies. The closer edge of the falls is bounded by a rocky, double ledge while the far end is framed by overhanging rhododendron and laurel scaling the steep, outer bank of the creek.

In hotter weather, after the waters warm a little, this is one of the better spots in the Smokies for a refreshing dip in the icy cold water of a mountain stream. The break in the forest cover around the pool makes this a premier swimming hole as the sun is able to warm the surrounding rocks where you will enjoy sunning as your body returns to 98.6 degrees. The rocky areas around Abrams Falls are also excellent for picnic outings. This is a popular destination, however, and often crowded.

After exploring the pool and its environs, simply retrace your steps to return to the parking area. 🏃🏃

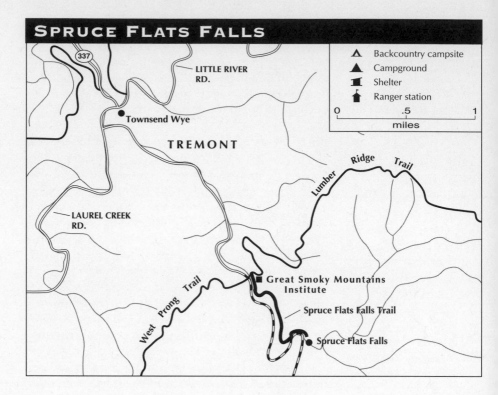

SPRUCE FLATS FALLS

337

LITTLE RIVER RD.

Townsend Wye

TREMONT

LAUREL CREEK RD.

Lumber Ridge Trail

West Prong Trail

Great Smoky Mountains Institute

Spruce Flats Falls Trail

Spruce Flats Falls

△ Backcountry campsite

▲ Campground

Shelter

Ranger station

0   .5   1
miles

Distance: 2.0 miles round-trip.

Elevation gain: 160 feet.

Brief trail description:
The trail to Spruce Flats Falls is a narrow, rugged course that winds along a high bluff overlooking the Middle Prong of the Little River. Along its highest point the trail affords fine opportunities for gazing into the deep river gorge below and across to the western end of the main Smoky Mountain divide in the distance. The trail ends in a steep descent to a rocky basin harboring a small pool at the foot of Spruce Flats Falls.

How to get there: From Sugarlands Visitor Center drive west on Little River Road 18.8 miles to Townsend Wye, or from Townsend, Tennessee, enter the Park and drive 1.0 mile to the Wye. From the Wye go west on Laurel Creek Road 0.2 mile to Tremont Road. Turn onto Tremont Road and proceed 2.2 miles to Great Smoky Mountains Institute and cross the bridge into the Institute compound. The trail to Spruce Flats Falls begins at the upper end of the road running through the compound.

0.0—Great Smoky Mountains Institute.

1.0—Spruce Flats Falls.

A deep, narrow gorge, guarded on one side by a sheer mountain slope and on the other by intersecting rows of staggered fortress-like cliffs, forms the channel in which the quick-running Spruce Flats Branch gathers momentum as it plunges over four separate precipices known collectively as the Spruce Flats Falls. The four are arranged consecutively, at varying intervals and increasing in height from upper to lower. The upper falls is hidden in a dark recess of the gorge, almost inaccessible. Seventy-five feet below, at a crook in the stream, is the second falls, a picturesque display of water plunging twenty feet onto a flat, rock basin from a rhododendron-cloistered notch in the cliff. The outer rim of the basin, only twenty feet from the base of the second falls, forms the edge of the third falls, a straight power plunge of nearly thirty feet onto a jumble of boulders. After flowing another hundred feet, the stream cascades forty feet into a deep, rock-rimmed pool.

This lesser-known jewel of the Smoky Mountains is reached by a rugged one-mile path that leaves from the upper end of the Great Smoky Mountains Institute in Tremont. The trail takes quickly up the adjoining ridge to a position high above the Middle Prong gorge. Here, in a strenuous fit of ups and downs, it edges along the rocky slopes above the river. At the top of the climb, the river can be seen far below, winding for several hundred yards through the mountain valley. A final, sharp descent heralds the approach to a plunge pool at the base of the lower falls.

Only the lower falls are clearly visible from the trail. The upper three falls are not easily accessed by following up the stream and thus are best seen by looking down on them from the top of the adjacent ridge. The trail continues across the creek in an exceedingly steep, two-hundred-yard series of switchbacks that lead to a wide, disused railroad berm running above the Spruce Flats Branch gorge. Part of each of the upper three falls can be

Spruce Flats Falls. Courtesy of Lou A. Murray.

seen from various vantage points along the railroad trace. Any approach to the three is extremely difficult as the intervening terrain is near vertical and heavily encumbered with cliffs, boulders, and rhododendron thickets. 🚶🚶

GROTTO FALLS

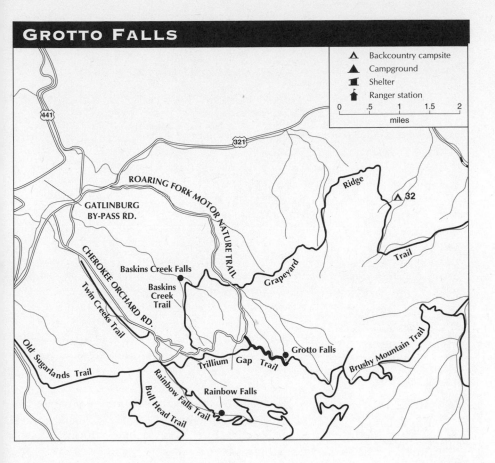

Legend:
- △ Backcountry campsite
- ▲ Campground
- ◪ Shelter
- ♜ Ranger station

0 .5 1 1.5 2
miles

441

321

ROARING FORK MOTOR NATURE TRAIL

GATLINBURG BY-PASS RD.

Ridge

△ 32

Trail

CHEROKEE ORCHARD RD.

Baskins Creek Falls

Baskins Creek Trail

Twin Creeks Trail

Grapeyard

Old Sugarlands Trail

Trillium Gap Trail

Grotto Falls

Brushy Mountain Trail

Rainbow Falls Trail

Rainbow Falls

Bull Head Trail

Distance: 2.4 miles round-trip.

Elevation gain: 500 feet.

Brief trail description:
The trail to Grotto Falls is a fine course for beginner hikers. The distance to the falls is fairly short, the grade is never steep, and the path is wide and not overly encumbered with rocks and roots. Because of its proximity to Gatlinburg, Grotto Falls is among the more heavily visited backcountry landmarks in the Park.

How to get there: Follow Airport Road 1.0 mile out of Gatlinburg into the Park. At the Park boundary the road's name changes to Cherokee Orchard Road. About 3.4 miles after entering the Park, the road becomes one-way. Just above this juncture, it passes the Rainbow Falls parking area on the right, then almost immediately passes a second parking area before approaching an intersection with the Roaring Fork Motor Nature Trail. The trail begins at the lower end of the Grotto Falls parking area, 2.0 miles along Roaring Fork Motor Nature Trail. (The Roaring Fork Motor Nature Trail is closed in winter).

0.0—Roaring Fork Motor Nature Trail (parking area).

0.1—Trillium Gap Trail leads in right from the Rainbow Falls Trail.

1.2—Grotto Falls.

From its base near Gatlinburg, Mount Le Conte rises over a mile high, making it the tallest mountain from base to summit east of the Mississippi. Over a course of six and a half miles, Roaring Fork descends from the top of Le Conte to Gatlinburg where it meets the West Prong of the Little Pigeon River, making it the steepest stream in the Smokies. Roaring Fork is graced by a continuous succession of falls, cascades, and plunge pools, the best known of which is Grotto Falls. The trail to Grotto Falls begins along the Roaring Fork Motor Nature Trail, a narrow winding road that plies the steep lower contours on the north side of Mount Le Conte.

Mount Le Conte was created by ancient geological upheavals that thrust the underlying rock strata upward at an angle of about 45 degrees to form the mountain's massive north face. As a result, the mountain imposes a considerable barrier to the oceans of moisture-laden air drifting across the Tennessee Valley, chilling it and precipitating the heavy rains that frequent the Smokies. This phenomenon largely accounts for the abundance of moisture found on the northern side of Le Conte.

In this cool moist environment, plant life exercises few constraints. All of the great trees of the Smokies are here: hemlocks, birches, buckeyes, maples, oaks, beeches, and silverbells. Higher up, above Grotto Falls, ancient enclaves of spruce and fir are interspersed with fire cherry and mountain ash. Squirrel-corn, trout lily, spring beauty, stinking Willie, black cohjosh, bishop's cap, bellwort, white and yellow violet, Fraser's sedge, great chickweed, and Solomon's seal are among the most common wildflowers on the lower slopes. In late April or very early May, many of these bloom simultaneously.

On leaving the Roaring Fork Motor Nature Trail, the trail to Grotto Falls follows a wide, well-marked course into the Roaring Fork drainage. The path's otherwise smooth surface is irregularly encumbered with occasional rocks and roots, and is crossed in a few places by small streams. The grade is never steep, making this a fine course for beginning hikers.

Although the trail's course is easy, the terrain itself is exceptionally rugged. Where the trail penetrates into hollows and stream drainages, the mountainside often drops away steeply from the trail's edge. Below, in the drainages, the mountain's rocky form is hidden by dense undergrowth.

As the trail approaches Grotto Falls, it enters into a narrow gorge that channels Roaring Fork. Here the mountain slopes steeply in from both sides, forcing the trail to the edge of the stream. After a short climb over a fairly rocky course, the trail reaches the back of the hollow where Roaring Fork rushes over a ledge and drops thirty feet onto the trail at Grotto Falls. Where the stream plunges onto the trail, the water collects momentarily in a shallow pool before seeping out and continuing down the mountain.

The name Grotto Falls is suggested by the space beneath the ledge over which the falls descend. The space is deep enough to permit hikers to pass behind the falls without getting wet. From beneath the falls the overhang of the ledge bears a slight resemblance to a shallow cave, thus the name Grotto Falls.

The area around Grotto Falls is severely confined by the stream gorge and does not afford attractive places for resting or eating lunch. There are a few suitable rocks on the far side of the stream, but these are unpleasantly close to the trail. As Grotto Falls is a popular destination in the Smokies, the area around them is often crowded.

While this hike ends at Grotto Falls, the trail itself continues another six and a half miles to the lodge at the summit of Mount Le Conte. 🚶🚶

Grotto Falls. Courtesy of Great Smoky Mountains National Park.

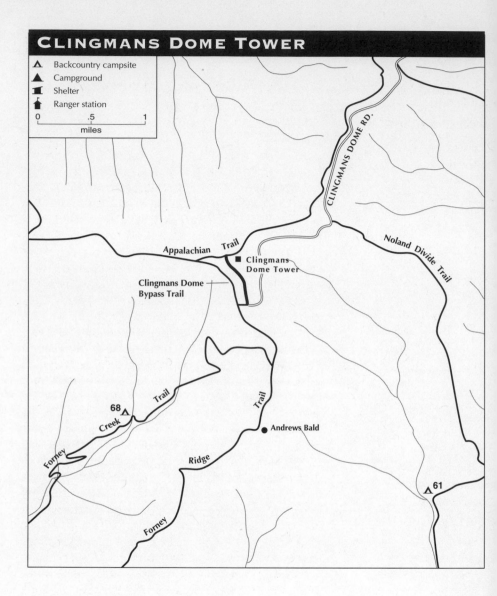

CLINGMANS DOME TOWER

△ Backcountry campsite
▲ Campground
🛏 Shelter
🚶 Ranger station

0   .5   1
miles

CLINGMANS DOME RD.

Noland Divide Trail

Appalachian Trail

■ Clingmans
Dome Tower

Clingmans Dome
Bypass Trail

Trail

68 △

Creek

Trail

Forney

● Andrews Bald

Ridge

△ 61

Forney

Distance: 1.0 mile round-trip.

Elevation gain: 335 feet.

Brief trail description:
The trail to the Clingmans Dome Tower is a wide paved track suitable for strollers and wheelchairs. Although its course is smooth and even, the grade is not always easy. Wooden benches are available at irregular intervals for those who want to pause and rest. At the summit of the dome, a modern tower provides one of the finest vantage points for surveying the greater Smoky Mountains environs. The deck of the tower is accessed by a wide gently sloping ramp. Rest-room facilities at the foot of the trail make this a convenient trail for families with small children.

How to get there: From Sugarlands Visitor Center, drive southeast on US 441 12.9 miles to Newfound Gap, or, from Oconaluftee Visitor Center, 15.9 miles northwest. At Newfound Gap, turn south onto Clingmans Dome Road and drive 7.0 miles to its end. The trail to Clingmans Dome Tower begins on the paved track next to the parking area.

0.0—Clingmans Dome Road (parking area).

0.1—Rest-room facilities.

0.5—Clingmans Dome Tower.

At 6,643 feet above sea level, Clingmans Dome is the highest peak in the Smokies, and second only to Mount Mitchell in North Carolina in being the highest east of the Mississippi. Before white settlers moved into the Smokies, this mountain was known by the Cherokee as Mulberry Place. According to legend, Mulberry Place was home of the White Bear, chief of all bears, and nearby was an enchanted lake where all animals could come for healing. Upon the arrival of the settlers the name "Mulberry Place" was superseded by "Smoky Dome," a name no doubt derived from the distinctive blue haze that often pervades the forest-clad ranges of the Smoky Mountains. During the mid-nineteenth century when scientific explorers first began venturing onto the higher peaks of the Smokies, Smoky Dome was re-named Clingmans Dome in honor of Thomas Lanier Clingman, a U.S. senator and Civil War general who actively promoted the virtues of the Great Smoky Mountains. Clingmans Dome is known principally today by hikers and tourists as the site of the Clingmans Dome Tower, one of the truly superb vantage points in the mountains.

When the first explorers ventured onto Clingmans Dome, they found its summit capped with dense thickets of Fraser fir generously interspersed with red spruce. The boles of the fir stands were so concentrated that one could see scarcely a few feet into the woods.

In the rarefied altitude of the upper peaks of the Smokies, the fir and spruce form a unique forest community that comprises a little more than 2 percent of the entire land area of the Park, and all of it is above 5,500 feet elevation. The old-growth spruce-fir stands like those on Clingmans Dome are relics from the time when the glaciers from the north exerted their chilling effects on the southern Appalachians. As the glaciers receded, the spruce and fir trees retreated north to

Canada and up to the highest peaks of the southern highlands. In the boreal coldness above 6,200 feet, healthy firs grow in pure stands, dark and dense, shutting out most undergrowth except for a few primitive mosses and lichens.

The firs are distinguished by their flat, blunt-tipped needles arranged along either side of the twigs, and a purplish cone that stands upright on the branches. In fall, the cone disintegrates, leaving a small spike on the branch. In Smoky Mountain vernacular, the firs were known as "she-balsams," evidently suggested by the white, resinous blisters on the bark of the trees that appear to be filled with milk.

The red spruce, colloquially known as the "he-balsam," is a tall, pagoda-shaped tree with stiff, spiky needles arranged thickly along all sides of the twigs. Unlike the firs, its cones hang down from the branches. Though a boreal species, the spruce is attracted to moisture and often is found along streamcourses below 4,000 feet elevation.

During the latter half of the twentieth century, the fir forests in the Smokies have been decimated by the invasion of the balsam woolly adelgid, a tiny sap-sucking aphid that burrows into the bark of the trees. Most of the mature fir forests have succumbed to the adelgid and are now just ghostly stands of dead-white boles. The firs regenerate prolifically but rarely reach maturity before being attacked by the adelgid. Botanists suspect that the demise of the fir tree is also having a weakening effect on the red spruce.

The trail to the tower passes through the dying fields of this once ancient and noble forest. Everywhere there are gray gaunt boles of the dead firs; in several places, however, the young firs have reestablished thickset stands reminiscent of the greater forest that once presided over the dome.

The flat summit of the dome harbors a forty-five-foot observation tower that affords one of the finest vantage points in the Smokies. The tower's observation deck is reached by a wide, gently sloping concrete ramp that circles up to the top. When the air is clear, the views from the tower are limitless in all directions. Particularly interesting are the massive south face of Mount Le Conte and the spine of the stateline divide in either direction.

Affixed at regular intervals around the tower's perimeter are framed photographs corresponding to the view from that position. Features on the photograph are labeled to assist the observer in identifying landmarks on the mountains.

Hikers wanting to add a little more adventure to their excursion to Clingmans Dome may wish to return to the parking area by a graded trail rather than the paved path. At the foot of the ramp to the tower a well-marked path leads twenty-five yards to the Appalachian Trail. From this junction, the Appalachian Trail leads left five hundred yards to an intersection with the Clingmans Dome Bypass Trail, which leads a half-mile back to the parking area. The Appalachian Trail at this point is a rugged little stretch that enters a fine section of spruce-fir forest. Upturned rock strata and gnarled roots make the walking surface uneven in places, though the grade is fairly level.

From its junction with the Appalachian Trail, the Clingmans Dome Bypass Trail is nearly all downhill. The path is somewhat rocky and often saturated with water seeping from the higher ground of the dome. Near its end, the trail intersects the upper terminus of the Forney Ridge Trail leading to Andrews Bald. At the junction, the Clingmans Dome Bypass Trail turns left and climbs shortly to the parking area. 🏃🏃

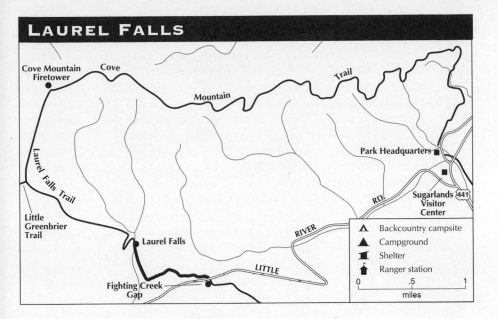

LAUREL FALLS

Cove Mountain Firetower

Cove

Mountain

Trail

Laurel Falls Trail

Little Greenbrier Trail

Park Headquarters

Sugarlands Visitor Center

RD.

441

Laurel Falls

RIVER

LITTLE

Fighting Creek Gap

	Backcountry campsite
	Campground
	Shelter
	Ranger station

0   .5   1

miles

LAUREL FALLS

Distance: 2.6 miles round-trip.

Elevation gain: 280 feet.

Brief trail description: The trail to Laurel Falls, one of the most popular in the Smokies, is a paved track that offers an easy excursion suitable for hikers accompanied by small children. The paved surface is sufficiently smooth to accommodate baby strollers and wheelchairs. The trail passes through a variety of forest cover, then follows a streamside course through a rugged gorge that leads to the edge of Laurel Falls. A flat, rocky apron at the base of the upper falls provides ample places to sit and enjoy the sights and sounds of rushing water.

How to get there: From the Sugarlands Visitor Center drive on Little River Road 3.7 miles west to Fighting Creek Gap. The trail to Laurel Falls begins on the right side of the road at the edge of the parking area.

0.0—Little River Road (parking area).

1.3—Laurel Falls.

The Laurel Falls Trail begins along the Little River Road at Fighting Creek Gap, so named not for some particular incident of physical combat in the neighborhood but for the long, continuous bickering about the location of a schoolhouse. The trail climbs immediately out of the gap and onto a paved track that begins tracing the gentle contours of the adjacent ridge. The trail maintains an easy grade that courses among pines and dry-ridge hardwoods. The paved track extends from Fighting Creek Gap to Laurel Falls, thus insuring that the path will be smooth and fairly dry.

About three quarters of a mile above Fighting Creek Gap, the trail climbs briefly, then turns and enters a rugged, steep-sided defile that channels Laurel Branch. Below, the stream can be heard rushing violently as it sluices through a pinched gorge known as the Devils Chute. From this point, until it reaches Laurel Falls, the trail remains high above the stream, tracing a level berm cut into the rock of the mountain slope by workers from the Civilian Conservation Corps. The steepness of the slope, the rushing stream, and the narrowness of the berm convey a sense of ruggedness, yet nowhere does the course pose any danger for the hiker.

A hundred yards or so into the stream gorge, the trail passes an opening in the forest cover that affords a clear view across the gorge to the higher mountain ranges to the south. The most prominent peak visible from the opening is Blanket Mountain, a rounded knob that punctuates the upper end of a long, steep ridge. Blanket Mountain was given its name by Return J. Meigs, an Indian commissioner who was charged with surveying these mountains following a treaty with the Cherokees. Meigs was attempting to retrace the boundary lines of the Indian land under a former treaty when his party became disoriented in a welter of high, rugged ridges. Meigs later commented that "the backwoodsman and the Indians could give us very little information, for neither had ever explored the great Iron Mountain [Smoky Mountains] anywhere near the part where the direction of our line would take us." In order to have a distinct target for his compass sights, Meigs had a brightly hued Indian blanket suspended from a high pole atop the mountain that has ever since been known as Blanket Mountain.

The trail penetrates into the deeper recesses of the gorge until eventually intersecting the stream at the narrow end of the defile where the stream drops across the trail at Laurel Falls. Laurel Branch drops forty feet over an uneven strata of ledges into a rock basin where it collects in a wide, shallow pool. Water from the pool spills over the basin's outer edge, dropping another forty feet before resuming its course as Laurel Branch.

The display of water at Laurel Falls is especially attractive when the stream is exceptionally high. Then, the basin is insufficient to pool the excess water and the stream literally spews off the lower falls. The lower falls can best be seen by circling through the amphitheater and proceeding downstream along the opposite side.

The paved trace stops at Laurel Falls, but the trail continues as a rocky course climbing out of the amphitheater and on to Cove Mountain. The trail crosses the falls on a narrow concrete pier that extends through the pool. During the colder seasons, spray from the falls freezes in thin layers on the rocky basin, making the area somewhat slick. 🚶

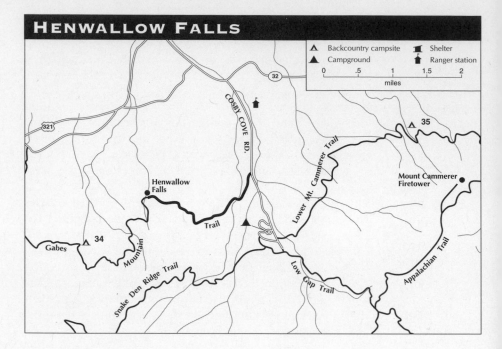

HENWALLOW FALLS

32

321

COSBY COVE RD.

△ 35

Henwallow
Falls

Lower Mt. Cammerer Trail

Mount Cammerer
Firetower

Trail

Gabes

△ 34

Mountain

Snake Den Ridge Trail

Low Gap Trail

Appalachian Trail

Distance: 4.2 miles round-trip.

Elevation gain: 800 feet.

Brief trail description: Henwallow Falls, the highest waterfall in the northeastern corner of the Park, is an exceptionally charming mountain landmark. The trail to Henwallow Falls is fairly easy and suitable for small children. Much of the area around Henwallow Falls is open woodland once occupied by mountaineer farms.

How to get there: From Gatlinburg drive east on US 321 to TN 32. Turn right and proceeds 0.8 mile to the entrance to Cosby Cove. From I-40 drive west to Cosby, then south on TN 32 to Cosby Cove. Turn right into Cosby Cove and drive 2.0 miles to the ranger station. Park behind the ranger station and walk back down the road 100 yards to the Cosby Cove Picnic Grounds. The trail to Henwallow Falls begins on the Gabes Mountain Trail across the road from the picnic grounds.

0.0—Cosby Picnic Grounds.

0.3—Junction. Trail leads in left from Cosby Campground.

1.1— Road turnaround.

2.1—Henwallow Falls.

Long before the advent of the Park, Henwallow Falls was a fashionable destination for Sunday drives and picnic lunches. In those days visitors to the falls would drive into Cosby Cove, then enter Bearneck Cove along an old wagon trace that passed several mountaineer settlements along the way. At the back of Bearneck Cove, they would leave their automobiles and walk a short distance to the falls along a settlers' path known then as the Messer Trail. Those with extra time and energy might venture further along the trail to enjoy the pockets of virgin forest that still grace the slopes above Henwallow Falls.

Since that time the settlement homes have been burned or torn down, the wagon road fallen into disuse, and the Messer Trail superseded by the graded Gabes Mountain Trail; nevertheless Henwallow Falls remains a popular destination for picnickers and day hikers.

The trail to Henwallow Falls follows the Gabes Mountain Trail beginning across the road from the Cosby Picnic Grounds near the Cosby Campground registration building. The trail proceeds into the woods about a quarter-mile before merging with a utility path leading in from the campground. Hikers staying at the campground can find this alternative access beginning along the paved road near the lower western corner of the campground.

At this juncture the trail strikes a westerly course across the tributaries of Crying Creek and into Bearneck Cove. Eventually the trail enters a clearing occupied by the remnant of a road turnaround. This road is part of the wagon trace used by visitors of yesteryear on their Sunday drive to Henwallow Falls. The trace runs back down the mountain and intersects the Cosby Cove access road a short distance below the picnic grounds.

The trail to Henwallow Falls continues at the back of the turnaround and climbs through open woods and into a small gap. Along this stretch are level plots marking former homesites, rock cairns, standing chimneys, and even a tiny cemetery. The trail continues through the gap, gradually gaining elevation, until reaching Messer Gap about a mile above the turnaround. On clearing Messer Gap, the trail drops quickly into the Lower Falling Branch drainage of Henwallow Creek. On the approach to the stream, a utility path exits right from the Gabes Mountain Trail and descends steeply two hundred yards to the foot of Henwallow Falls. Here the stream is shunted into a narrow aperture at the brink of a sixty-foot cliff; then, squeezing through the opening, it fans out quickly into a shimmering cascade that rolls down the bare face of the cliff wall.

According to a bit of tradition preserved by Carson Brewer in *Hiking in the Great Smokies,* the name "Henwallow" is the result of an act of spite on the part of one community toward another. It appears that a family living in a small, unnamed

Henwallow Falls. Courtesy of Great Smoky Mountains National Park.

community near here had, one spring, ordered one hundred baby chicks from a hatchery. The family had intended to raise the chicks to egg-laying hens and sell their eggs. When the chickens became old enough for their gender to be obvious, the family counted ninety-five roosters and five pullets. People in another nearby, unnamed community, thinking this was rather funny, took to calling the first community Roostertown. The folks in Roostertown, unappreciative of their new name, responded by calling the first community Henwallow. There was no basis for the name; it was strictly an act of revenge.

As a footnote, today the former locations of Henwallow and Roostertown are unknown, but both survive in Smoky Mountain nomenclature, although Roostertown occurs as the name of a road off US 321 just outside the Park boundary. 🏃🏃

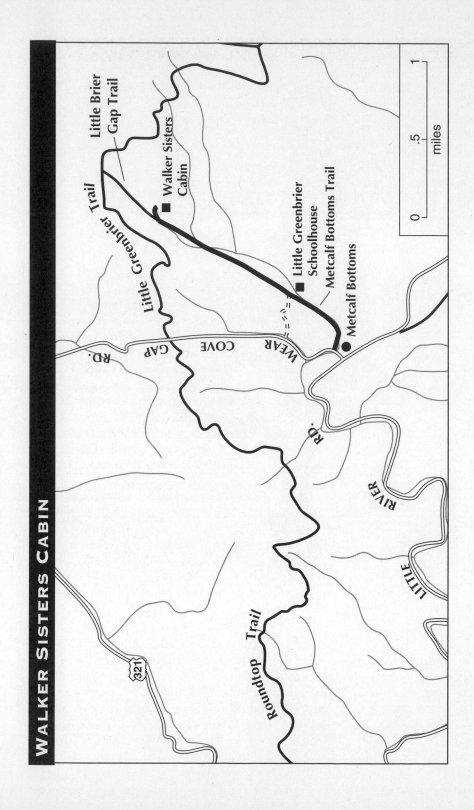

Little Brier
Gap Trail

Walker Sisters
Cabin

Little Greenbrier Trail

Little Greenbrier
Schoolhouse

Metcalf Bottoms Trail

Metcalf Bottoms

WEAR COVE

GAP RD.

RD.

RIVER

LITTLE

Roundtop Trail

321

0   .5   1
miles

Distance: 3.6 miles round-trip.

Elevation gain: 360 feet.

Brief trail description:
The Walker Sisters Cabin is one of the few examples of primitive Appalachian architecture remaining in the Smokies. It stands in Five Sisters Cove, an enclosed hollow about two miles above Metcalf Bottoms on Little River. The trail to the cabin follows initially along the Metcalf Bottoms Trail which begins at the perimeter of the Metcalf Bottoms Picnic Grounds where the Wear Cove Gap Road crosses the bridge over Little River. The Metcalf Bottoms Trail terminates in one mile at the Little Greenbrier Schoolhouse, and a well-maintained gravel road continues from the schoolhouse another mile to the cabin. The entire course from Metcalf Bottoms through the schoolyard to Five Sisters Cove is fairly level.

How to get there: From the Sugarlands Visitor Center drive west along the Little River Road 9.5 miles to the Metcalf Bottoms Picnic Grounds, or from the Townsend Wye, east 9.3 miles. The trail to the Walker Sisters Cabin follows the Metcalf Bottoms Trail beginning at the far end of the bridge over Little River.

0.0—Metcalf Bottoms.

0.6—Little Greenbrier Schoolhouse.

1.6—Road into Five Sisters Cove.

1.8—Walker Sisters Cabin.

The trail to the Walker Sisters Cabin leaves Metcalf Bottoms and follows Little River upstream one hundred yards to where it turns and charts an easy, half-mile stream-side course up Little Greenbrier Branch to the Little Greenbrier Schoolhouse. The houses and farms that once dotted Metcalf Bottoms are gone, but the trail has probably changed very little since the time children from around the Little River valley walked this way to school. The Little Greenbrier Schoolhouse is a one-room log cabin constructed of massive poplar timbers and bearing a split-shingle roof. The schoolhouse is sparsely furnished with wooden benches arranged irregularly across a raised board floor.

The schoolhouse was completed and opened for classes on January 1, 1882, but the building was considered too valuable a community asset to be used solely as a school, and so it also saw service as a church until a proper church building was erected nearby in 1924. The church building no longer stands on this spot, but the cemetery remains just above the schoolyard.

The Little Greenbrier Schoolhouse can also be reached by automobile over a one-lane gravel road leaving the Wear Cove Gap Road just above Metcalf Bottoms. On reaching the schoolhouse, the road continues another mile into Little Greenbrier Cove and terminates at the Walker Sisters Cabin. A gate blocks the road at the school. This gate marks the lower terminus of the Little Brier Gap Trail.

For its first three-quarters of a mile, the Little Brier Gap Trail follows the gravel road to the cabin. The road's course is straight, level, and impeded only by one significant stream crossing. The trail and road part company where the road turns sharply right and enters Five Sisters Cove, named for the Walker sisters, Margaret, Polly, Martha, Louisa, and Hettie, who steadfastly maintained their bustling mountaineer homestead in this cove until the last of them died in 1964.

The Walker Sisters Cabin, one of a very few original mid-nineteenth-century log structures remaining in the Park, stands at the end of the road. The cabin is a three-room, two-story building with a front porch running the length of the kitchen. It looks now as it did in the 1870s when it was built.

Brice McFalls is thought to have made the first improvements in the cove in the 1840s, building a cabin about four hundred yards from the Walker home. Wiley King, a grandfather of the sisters, later built another cabin in the cove. It was completed by his sons the year after King's death in 1859.

According to the research monograph *Mountain Home* by Robert R. Madden and T. Russell Jones, John N. Walker married Wiley King's daughter, Margaret Jane, in 1866 and moved with his family into the King cabin in the 1870s. The expanding Walker family soon outgrew the house, and John was forced to dismantle the old McFalls cabin and use it as a kitchen addition to his house. He also added the porch at the same time.

Over the years, John Walker constructed numerous outbuildings around the house. These included a barn, a pig pen, a corn crib-gear shed, a smokehouse, an applehouse, a springhouse, a blacksmith shop, a grist mill, and a poultry yard. One building conspicuously absent was the outhouse. The Walker family used the woods, with the women using those below the house and the men those above. Of these buildings, only the springhouse and corn crib-gear shed remain.

Walker also constructed a tar kiln, ash hopper, charcoal-making pit, drying racks, bee gums, and rail and stone fences. He planted orchards of apple, plum, cherry, peach, and chestnut trees and cleared land for a garden and corn patch.

When John Walker died, five of his daughters remained on the farm, continuing the Smoky Mountain tradition of self-reliance with an unfailing adherence to the value of hard work instilled in them by their parents. 🏃🏃

BASKINS CREEK FALLS

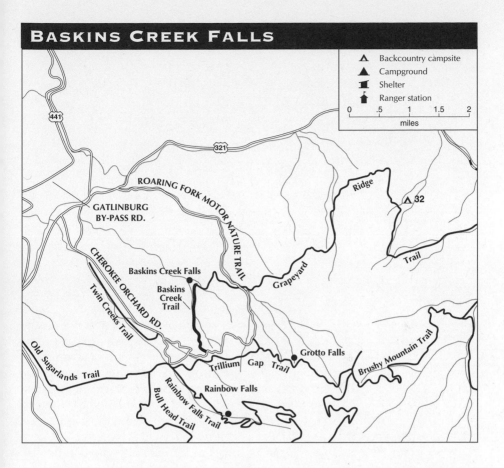

Legend:
- Backcountry campsite
- Campground
- Shelter
- Ranger station

0   .5   1   1.5   2
miles

441

321

ROARING FORK MOTOR NATURE TRAIL

GATLINBURG
BY-PASS RD.

CHEROKEE ORCHARD RD.

Twin Creeks Trail

Baskins Creek Falls

Baskins
Creek
Trail

Grapeyard

Ridge

Trail

△ 32

Old Sugarlands Trail

Trillium   Gap   Trail

Grotto Falls

Brushy Mountain Trail

Rainbow Falls Trail

Rainbow Falls

Bull Head Trail

BASKINS CREEK FALLS

Distance: 3.8 miles round-trip.

Elevation loss: 670 feet.

Brief trail description:
The trail to Baskins Creek Falls is an ideal course for those wanting to avoid the usual haunts and venture into one of the more infrequently visited sections of the Smokies. The trail is marked and well graded. Except for a steep descent into the falls' amphitheater, the course is moderately easy to hike. The trail's most prominent landmark is Baskins Creek Falls, one of the lesser-known jewels of the Smokies.

How to get there: Follow the Airport Road 1.0 mile out of Gatlinburg into the Park. At the Park boundary the road continues, but the name changes to Cherokee Orchard Road. About 3.4 miles after entering the Park, the road becomes one-way at the Rainbow Falls parking area. Continue on Cherokee Orchard Road another 0.5 mile to its intersection with the Roaring Fork Motor Nature Trail. Park at the intersection and walk 350 yards up the Roaring Fork Motor Nature Trail. The Baskins Creek Trail begins along the left side of the road. On the right, another trail leads to the Trillium Gap Trail and Grotto Falls. (The Roaring Fork Motor Nature Trail is closed to vehicular traffic between December 1 and March 31.)

0.0—Roaring Fork Motor Nature Trail (parking area).

1.2—Path leads left 350 yards to the Baskins Cemetery.

1.6—Path leads left 450 yards to Baskins Creek Falls.

1.9—Baskins Creek Falls.

 Placenames in the Great Smoky Mountains are known for their charm, colorfulness, and descriptive flavor. Often they were the result of a spontaneous application commemorating some local incident that made a lasting impression on the mountaineers. The remembered incident may have entailed an element of tragedy or humor, of local custom, or perhaps of some unexpected good fortune on a bear or turkey hunt. In some cases placenames were suggested by the wildlife inhabiting a certain ridge or hollow, and in others by a peculiar physical feature in the immediate vicinity. The legacies of pioneer settlers and intrepid explorers were also often memorialized in Smoky Mountain placenames.

Many of the original placenames survived, some were lost, and others were corrupted into unrecognizable derivatives. Baskins Creek on the lower north slope of Mount Le Conte is an example of how an original name underwent change.

According to early Smoky Mountain lore, a noted bear hunter named Joe built for himself a cabin above Gatlinburg along a small stream. The bear hunter trafficked in bearskins and was thus known as Bearskin Joe, and the stream by which he lived came to be called Bearskin Joe's Creek. For the sake of brevity and less awkwardness, the "Joe" was soon dropped from the creek's name. A slurring of the pronunciation shortened the name still further until it reached its present form.

In Bearskin Joe's time, cabins and farms ranged along Baskins Creek from its headwaters on Piney Mountain to its mouth on the Little Pigeon River in Gatlinburg. Trails leading out of the Baskins Creek drainage connected the cabins with Cherokee Orchard, Spruce Flats, Roaring Fork, and other communities in the vicinity. The present Baskins Creek Trail traces the course of old trails entering from the upper end of the Baskins Creek valley.

On leaving the Roaring Fork Motor Nature Trail, the Baskins Creek Trail climbs easily up and over an extended finger ridge of Piney Mountain through a cut-over forest of pines and dry-ridge hardwoods. For the first half-mile the course follows an uneven up-and-down cadence before turning and descending into the Falls Branch drainage. The rate of descent accelerates as the trail enters an enclosed cove dotted with scattered patches of rhododendron crowding the banks of Falls Branch.

Near the bottom of the cove, a spur exits sharply back left and leads across Falls Branch and to a primitive cemetery perched on a small knoll four hundred yards above the main trail. The tiny cemetery bears a little more than a dozen graves marked with thin tablets of stone worn nearly free of their hand-etched inscriptions.

Baskins Creek Falls.
Courtesy of Lou A.
Murray.

Beyond the junction leading to the cemetery, the trail continues through the cove another three hundred yards to a second intersection. Here another spur exits left and follows Falls Branch on a remarkably level course one quarter-mile to the Baskins Creek Falls. (The main trail climbs quickly out of the cove then turns sharply back to the Roaring Fork Motor Nature Trail.)

The final approach to Baskins Creek Falls, however, is marked by a very steep descent to the base of a great sandstone bluff. Fortress-like, this imposing edifice guards the upper end of a remarkably open, flat-bottomed hollow. Near the center of the amphitheater, Falls Branch flows over the upper edge of the bluff and drops thirty-five feet to form the Baskins Creek Falls.

The water from the falls does not pool at the base of the bluff but gathers quickly into a stream and runs off into a small, grassy field at the bottom of the hollow. At the falls, a manway crosses the stream and wanders down to the field, where it again crosses at the confluence of Falls Branch and Baskins Creek. Technically the waterfall is on Falls Branch and not Baskins Creek; however, given its proximity to the parent stream, it is popularly known as Baskins Creek Falls.

The field below the falls is a fine place to take a picnic lunch and bask in the sun while enjoying the solitude of the mountains and the gentle roar of the falls. 🏃

Day Hikes

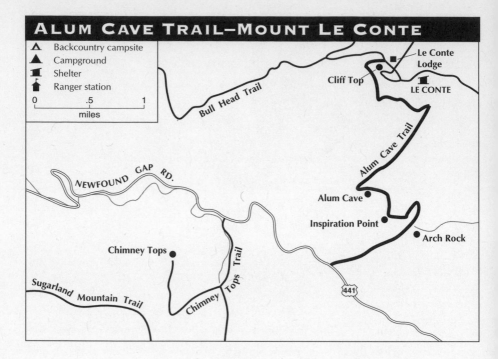

ALUM CAVE TRAIL—MOUNT LE CONTE

△ Backcountry campsite
▲ Campground
⬛ Shelter
⬛ Ranger station

0   .5   1
miles

Bull Head Trail

Le Conte Lodge

Cliff Top

LE CONTE

Alum Cave Trail

NEWFOUND GAP RD.

Alum Cave

Inspiration Point

Arch Rock

Chimney Tops

Chimney Tops Trail

441

Sugarland Mountain Trail

ALUM CAVE TRAIL–MOUNT LE CONTE

Distance: 10.2 miles round-trip.

Elevation gain: 2,560 feet.

Brief trail description: The Alum Cave Trail to Mount Le Conte is arguably the finest hiking trail in the Smokies. No trail of comparable distance affords quite the panoply of notable landmarks, scenic overlooks, and unusual geological features as does this trail. The trail is fairly level to Arch Rock, then becomes markedly steeper. Higher up the conditions are rougher. Here the trail crosses several narrow ledges and rocky places made slick by seepage from the adjacent slopes.

How to get there: Drive to the Alum Cave parking area on the Newfound Gap Road 8.6 miles southeast of the Sugarlands Visitor Center, or 4.3 miles northwest of Newfound Gap. The trail begins along the gravel path adjacent to the parking area.

0.0—Grassy Patch (parking area).

1.4—Arch Rock.

1.5—Huggins Hell.

1.8—Inspiration Point.

2.3—Alum Cave Bluff.

5.0—Rainbow Falls Trail leads right to Mount Le Conte.

5.1—Le Conte Lodge.

The lower half of the Alum Cave Trail to Mount Le Conte, which includes the stretch between the Grassy Patch and Alum Cave Bluff, is covered in the Alum Cave Bluff narrative in the Short Hikes section of this book. This narrative begins from the upper end of Alum Cave Bluff.

On leaving Alum Cave, the trail loops up and around the bluff and follows the ridge which forms the southern flank of Mount Le Conte. Where openings in the trees permit, the rock faces of Cliff Top along the southern edge of Mount Le Conte are visible to the left. To the right, Peregrine Peak, a cone-shaped slick rises straight up from the floor of Huggins Hell.

An abrupt turn to the left marks the point where the trail leaves the ridge and begins cutting across the mountain face underneath the wide summit of Mount Le Conte. In several places the trail, chiseled out of solid rock, edges its way along narrow ledges. The grade here is very slight and, where there is any danger at all, the trail is equipped with cable handrails.

Along this stretch there is a marked change in vegetation. The woods open up and the rhododendron scatter. The spruce, which are most abundant on the intermediate ridges, yield to the fir trees. In addition, clumps of shrub-like sand myrtle cling to the small crags flaring out from the cliff sides.

Near the summit, the trail circles wide right to clear the western end of Cliff Top. A silent stand of boreal forest, dark and closely growing balsams, encroaches on the trail. Moss and wood sorrel hide the spongy, age-old, forest floor. This particular vegetation, with its sweet resinous aroma, appears only in the higher elevations of the Smokies and in the Canadian tundra.

Two hundred yards shy of its terminus at Le Conte Lodge, the trail is joined from the left by the Rainbow Falls Trail. The trail terminates along the upper edge of the lodge at an intersection with the Boulevard Trail, approaching from the east, and a spur leading up the hill to Cliff Top, one of the peaks of Mount Le Conte.

Le Conte Lodge is a hostel compound consisting of several wood-shingled cabins, two lodges, a dining room, and two outhouses. There is no electricity, and water is pumped into holding tanks from nearby Basin Spring. The lodge is situated in a bench or basin on the north slope about a quarter-mile below Cliff Top. Drinking water is available at two spigots located outside the cabins.

The area around the lodge offers fine opportunities for seeing bears in the wild, and there are endless bear stories, some more true than others, that originate on Mount Le Conte. One of our favorites involves two mother bears who, twenty years ago, had four or five cubs between them. It seems that they had figured out how to get their claws under a cabin door and pull it open. One would break into a cabin while the other watched the "children."

In the 1980s there was a resident bear with the unusual name of "Boomerang." Boomerang acquired her name when a research team shot her with a tranquilizer dart and she took off running. She ran around the lodge site until she ended up right back at their feet in a trance. After she was tagged, she remained on Le Conte and raised several litters of cubs.

Mount Le Conte is generally considered to have four peaks. From east to west these are Myrtle Point, High Top, Cliff Top, and West Point. High Top and West Point are completely covered with trees and offer no views. Immediately above Le Conte Lodge is Cliff Top, one of the premier vantage points in the Smokies. Cliff Top is covered with dense stands of windswept balsams and scattered rhododendron. Its precipitous south side is draped in masses of billowy sand myrtle which, in mid-June, yield rich pink and white blossoms.

More often than not, the view from Cliff Top is obscured by swirling, misty clouds. Below, vague shapes of mountains appear only to vanish and reappear. When the sky is clear, Cliff Top offers a superb view of Sugarland valley, the vast chasm that separates Mount Le Conte from the main Smoky Mountain range. To the west lies the Tennessee Valley and, in the distance, the dim edge of the Cumberland Plateau.

The uppermost point on Mount Le Conte, High Top, is 6,593 feet above sea level, more than a mile above the mountain's base near Gatlinburg. The mile distance from base to summit makes Mount Le Conte the tallest mountain east of the Mississippi. High Top is along the Boulevard Trail about one half-mile east of Le Conte Lodge. Tradition has it that hikers are to toss a rock onto the pile marking High Top in deference to an old Cherokee superstition of offering a rock to appease the evil spirits.

Myrtle Point, because of its northern and eastern exposure, is the premier spot in the Smokies for watching the sunrise. Named for the ubiquitous sand myrtle, Myrtle Point is actually a platform-like protrusion astride a razor-thin section of the

Boulevard. The view to the south is similar to that from Cliff Top except that Myrtle Point affords a clear look down the maw of Huggins Hell. The view to the north is wide and spacious, encompassing the rugged environs of Greenbrier Cove and its guardian, Greenbrier Pinnacle, marked by the distinctive lines of cliffs on its western end.

Both Myrtle Point and Cliff Top afford ample space to sit out on the rocks and enjoy a picnic lunch while surveying the vast expanse of beautiful mountains. After lunch, you may return by the Alum Cave Trail or, if provisions for a shuttle have been made, along one of four other trails descending Le Conte. The Boulevard Trail descends east to Newfound Gap, along the tortuous ridge that connects Mount Le Conte with the main Smoky Mountain divide. On the east side of Le Conte are the Bull Head and Rainbow Falls Trails which terminate near one another in Cherokee Orchard above Gatlinburg. And, along the wet, lush north slope, the Trillium Gap Trail descends to the Roaring Fork Motor Nature Trail or, following the Brushy Mountain alternative, to Greenbrier Cove. 🏃

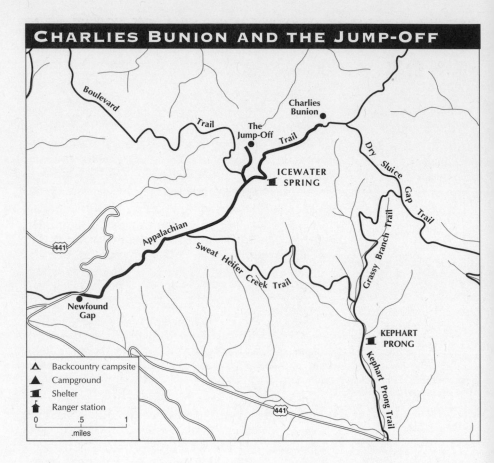

CHARLIES BUNION AND THE JUMP-OFF

Boulevard

Trail

Charlies
Bunion

The
Jump-Off

Trail

Dry Sluice Gap Trail

ICEWATER
SPRING

Appalachian

441

Sweat Heifer Creek Trail

Grassy Branch Trail

Newfound
Gap

KEPHART
PRONG

Kephart Prong Trail

441

▲ Backcountry campsite

▲ Campground

Shelter

Ranger station

0   .5   1

.miles

Distance: 8.2 miles round-trip.

Elevation gain: 1,200 feet.

Brief trail description:
The trail to Charlies Bunion is one of the busiest in the Smokies. It follows the Appalachian Trail east out of Newfound Gap and stays generally to the crest of the main divide. The trail is reasonably easy to hike although there are some steep, rocky places near each end of the trail. The trail to the Jump-Off is an unmaintained 0.6 mile manway that begins near the intersection of the Appalachian Trail and the Boulevard, and climbs to the summit of Mount Kephart. The manway is well marked but somewhat rugged.

How to get there: The trail to Charlies Bunion and the Jump-Off begins in Newfound Gap on US 441 (Newfound Gap Road) about 13 miles southeast of the Sugarlands Visitor Center near Gatlinburg or about 15 miles northwest of the Oconaluftee Visitor Center near Cherokee, North Carolina. The trailhead is in the northeast corner of the parking lot, near the rest rooms.

0.0—Newfound Gap.

1.7—Sweat Heifer Trail leads right.

2.8—Boulevard Trail leads left (trail to Jump-Off).

3.1—Icewater Spring Shelter.

3.2—Icewater Spring.

4.1—Charlies Bunion.

The trail to Charlies Bunion and the Jump-Off is one of the few in the Smokies that offers spectacular panoramic views at both its beginning and end. The trail's lower end is anchored in Newfound Gap, overlooking the vast upper reaches of the Oconaluftee Valley. The trail's upper end leads to Charlies Bunion and the Jump-Off, two of the more spectacular vantage points in the Smokies.

Before the advent of the Park, Newfound Gap was an insignificant swag in the Smokies crest, not even distinguished by a trail. The gap was eventually widened to make room for the transmountain highway, now known as the Newfound Gap Road. When the highway was completed, a rock-work platform was built into the slope on the north side of the gap and served as a dais when President Franklin D. Roosevelt officially dedicated the Great Smoky Mountains National Park in 1940.

The trail begins at the rock-works and follows the Appalachian Trail northeast out of Newfound Gap. The grade is moderate and the trail's footing a bit rocky in places. There are no views along this initial stretch except where the forest cover opens momentarily for glimpses of the amorphous layers of the distant North Carolina ranges.

A half-mile above Newfound Gap, the rocky course grades into a broad fairway that extends along the stateline divide to the foot of Mount Kephart. Though the path is wet in spots, the hiking here is like strolling through a great open park of large spruce and birch with little undergrowth except for a carpet of thick mountain grass. At several intervals, short side-paths lead up to the ridgeline, offering views of the North Carolina mountains.

Except for a brief climb or two, the path is disturbed only by the Sweat Heifer Trail intersecting from the right. Otherwise it continues in a leisurely manner, arriving after another mile at the base of Mount Kephart and a junction marking the lower terminus of the Boulevard Trail. Here, the trail to the Jump-Off goes left, following the Boulevard Trail, and the trail to Charlies Bunion goes right following the Appalachian Trail.

The trail to the Jump-Off is a well-maintained manway that exits right from the Boulevard Trail one hundred feet beyond the junction with the Appalachian Trail. It runs about one half-mile over the summit of Mount Kephart and out to the Jump-Off. Prior to reaching the Jump-Off, the manway levels briefly for a fine view of the east edge of Mount Le Conte and the Boulevard, the crooked, razor-thin ridge that connects Mount Le Conte with the main Smoky divide. From this perspective, all of the peaks of Mount Le Conte are visible. To the right of Le Conte is the conspicuous pale verdure of Brushy Mountain, a heath bald that graces the long northern flank of Mount Le Conte.

Mount Kephart, like many peaks in the Smokies, offers no view from its highest point. The Jump-Off serves, much as Myrtle Point and the Cliff Top do for Mount Le Conte, as the vantage point from Mount Kephart. The east edge of the Jump-Off is a vertical cliff that drops one thousand feet into a vast gulf. In the Smokies, only the Chimneys and Greenbrier Pinnacle compare with the precarious edge.

The steep south wall of the gulf is formed by the stateline divide meandering to an indeterminate point in the east with Laurel Top, Mount Chapman, and Mount Guyot arrayed prominently along its crest. The far end of the gulf is defined by Greenbrier Pinnacle, the massive lead that ends abruptly over Greenbrier Cove. Behind the Pinnacle is the distinctive anvil-shaped English Mountain.

To the left, rising from the bottom of the gulf is Horseshoe Mountain, named for its concave shape. And, prominent in the immediate distance to the right, is a grotesque rock promontory, Charlies Bunion.

The naming of Charlies Bunion is an odd piece of Smoky Mountain lore. In 1929, a resident of Oconaluftee named Charlie Conner led a party trying to locate and name known topographical features. The group included Horace Kephart, the noted author of *Our Southern Highlanders*. While crossing a small knoll, Conner's feet began hurting. He complained to his companions of his hurting feet, mentioning something about a bunion. Later, while standing at the Jump-Off and surveying the rugged Tennessee slopes, Conner pointed to an unnamed hump on the stateline divide and said "That's just about like my bunion," or words to that effect.

"Then we'll call it Charlies Bunion," replied Kephart, and the name became a fixture in Smoky Mountain nomenclature.

The trail to Charlies Bunion begins back at the intersection of the Boulevard and the Appalachian Trail. At this juncture, the Appalachian Trail leaves the ridge and proceeds around the North Carolina side of Mount Kephart, descending shortly to the Icewater Spring Shelter, a stone structure sitting comfortably on a broad, rolling knoll just below the trail. This setting is among the finest of all the shelter sites in the Park. The area is open, level, and carpeted in thick grass.

On the summer solstice several years ago, a group of us pulled into Icewater Spring to spend the night. When we arrived, we were greeted by a lone camper, an irascible tattooed old man named Denver whose vocabulary was limited mostly to four-letter words. At the time, the shelter also included two permanent residents, Priscilla and Elvis, a pair of skunks who made their home under the first tier of bunks and emerged every evening around dinner time to share a good fire and a hearty meal with the hikers.

The next morning, one of the authors, heeding the call of nature, leaned his pack against a post outside the shelter, grabbed a roll of toilet paper, and headed down to the woods below the shelter.

"On the way back I looked up and saw my companions standing behind the fence enclosing the shelter, jumping and shouting. I noticed that my pack had been moved and that Denver was standing in the camp yard trying to take my picture. What I could not see was a large bear walking through the high grass on a path perpendicular to mine. The bear, like I, was focused on the picture-taking Denver and the confusion in the shelter, and was unaware of my approach.

At the point where our paths intersected, the bear and I bumped into one another. I jumped straight up. The bear, equally startled, bounded off in a heavy gallop. Ten yards away, he stopped and turned around. We looked at each other briefly before the bear turned quickly and ambled off down the mountainside.

Charlies Bunion. Courtesy of Great Smoky Mountains National Park.

Beyond Icewater Spring, the trail descends about two miles along a rough course that leads to the foot of Charlies Bunion. The Bunion is an association of stark cliffs, ramparts, and jagged ridges scorched black in a 1925 forest fire that swept up and over the mountain from the North Carolina slope. Prior to the fire, the Bunion area was densely matted with a spongy humus and shaded by closely growing fir, leaving few visible traces of the rock beneath. Four years after the fire, a thunderstorm plowed into the mountain, sending a flood of rainwater onto the burned-over Bunion. During the deluge, the once-burnt, water-soaked earth lost its grip and slid into the steep ravine below, carrying with it all the vegetation and leaving nothing but bare rock behind. The tree trunks swept away in the flood are still visible, piled like kindling in the narrow defiles a thousand feet below.

On Labor day 1951, a second flood washed out the thin vegetation that had managed to regain a tenuous hold on the scoured rock. Today the Bunion is still largely bare, dotted only with a few clumps of sand myrtle, and remaining, as veteran hiker Harvey Broome once suggested, as "a barren monument to man's carelessness with fire and nature's excess with water."

From the top of Charlies Bunion looking into the ravine a naked, razor-thin spine is prominent, extending like a buttress between the base of the Bunion and a small knob. The sides of the spine are appallingly steep, falling sharply away to the ravine below. The Bunion and its immediate environs are unparalleled examples of the rugged eastern Smokies.

The geography observable from Charlies Bunion is essentially the same as that from the Jump-Off. ; however, the perspective is totally different. Charlies Bunion lacks the long panorama down the stateline divide and the sheer sense of depth of the Jump-Off. The Bunion offers a more accommodating resting place. Its rocky outcropping is ideally situated for a leisurely picnic lunch while gazing out over the immense forested valley below and watching the hawks that frequently glide on the updrafts while searching for prey. 🏃🏃

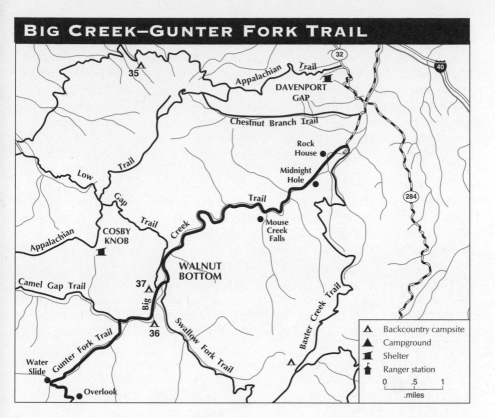

BIG CREEK–GUNTER FORK TRAIL

32

40

35

Appalachian   Trail

DAVENPORT
GAP

Chestnut Branch Trail

Rock
House

Midnight
Hole

Low   Trail

284

Gap

Trail   Trail

Appalachian

COSBY
KNOB

Creek

Mouse
Creek
Falls

WALNUT
BOTTOM

Camel Gap Trail

37

Big

36

Baxter Creek Trail

Swallow Fork Trail

Water
Slide

Gunter Fork Trail

Overlook

◬	Backcountry campsite
▲	Campground
▛	Shelter
⛽	Ranger station

0   .5   1
.miles

Big Creek–Gunter Fork Trail

Distance: 16.4 miles round-trip.

Elevation gain: 3,680 feet.

Brief trail description: The Big Creek Trail is a wonderful hike for those who wish to avoid the rigors of a steep climb yet still enjoy the ruggedness of the Smoky Mountains. This trail is a gentle incline that follows an old railroad grade into an enclosed boulder-strewn basin. Its course wanders through one of the more remote areas of the Smokies and thus affords a fine opportunity for mountain solitude. Big Creek, one of the more picturesque streams in the Smokies, is liberally dotted with falls, plunge pools, and waterslides.

How to get there: Drive on I-40 60 miles east from Knoxville or 50 miles west from Asheville to the Waterville exit. Cross the Pigeon River and follow the road upstream to the Carolina Power and Light Company. At the power plant, the road turns and proceeds 2.0 miles to an intersection with old NC 284 at the Mount Sterling community. Pass through the intersection. The Big Creek ranger station is 0.2 mile along the road. The Big Creek Trail begins on the right 0.7 mile beyond the ranger station. Parking is available just below the trailhead, near the picnic area.

0.0—Big Creek Road (parking area).

1.0—Rock House.

1.4—Midnight Hole.

2.0—Mouse Creek Falls.

2.8—Brakeshoe Spring.

5.2—Walnut Bottom. Swallow Fork Trail leads left.

5.4—Lower Walnut Bottom Backcountry Campsite. Lowe Gap Trail leads right.

5.7—Upper Walnut Bottom Backcountry Campsite.

5.8—Big Creek Trail grades in the Camel Gap Trail.

6.4—Gunter Fork Trail leads left.

6.5—Wet crossing of Big Creek.

7.8—Gunter Fork Cascade.

8.2—Water slide.

The first two miles of this hike are covered in the short hike to Midnight Hole. This narrative begins at Mouse Creek Falls.

About a quarter of a mile above Mouse Creek Falls, the trail shoots across a sturdy bridge above another of the many pools on Big Creek. The trail and creek trace the keel of the basin for the next two miles, making the rushing stream a welcome and noisy companion.

About a half-mile above the bridge crossing, a small spring cascades over a mossy stone to the left of the trail. Earlier in the century, an engineer from a logging train placed a locomotive brakeshoe on the rock just below the spring to capture the water. Passersby soon named the spot Brakeshoe Spring, and the substantial iron shoe remained in its place for fifty years until some unthinking souvenir hunter stole it sometime in the mid-1970s.

About three miles above Brakeshoe Spring the trail is marked by the lower terminus of the Swallow Fork Trail near the entrance to Walnut Bottom, a way station on the old railroad line. Two hundred yards past this junction, the trail crosses a bridge and passes by the first of two very hospitable campsites. The first campsite (37) anchors the lower end of Walnut Bottom and the second (36), a half-mile upstream, marks its upper end. Just beyond the first site the Low Gap Trail forks right on its way up and over the Appalachian Trail to the Cosby Campground.

A hundred yards beyond the upper Walnut Bottom camp the Big Creek Trail grades into the Camel Gap Trail. A sign near this point marks the Gunter Fork Trail branching off to the left. From the Camel Gap Trail the Gunter Fork Trail immediately crosses Big Creek in a wide ford. The water is cold and, after a good rain, the stream can be deep and swift.

On the far side of Big Creek, the trail proceeds through old farm fields and requires several rock hops as it crisscrosses Gunter Fork. About one and a half miles above the Gunter Fork trailhead, at a sharp left turn in the trail, a path leads right, downhill, to the Gunter Fork Cascade. The cascade is a ten-foot drop by Gunter Fork over a cliff edge into a shallow pool. The cascade is not very powerful, but the setting for the falls is quite attractive.

About five hundred yards and a couple of easy stream crossings, further along, the trail passes the foot of a two-hundred-foot water slide. This is truly an impressive piece of rock. At the top, a thin sheet of water scoots over a dome-shaped edge and drops twenty feet onto a long water slide. As it descends, the water fans out along the rock face before falling into a small pool beside the trail.

Just beyond this point, the trail crosses the stream a final time before starting a fairly strenuous climb to Balsam Mountain. If you have the time and the extra energy, it is worth hiking up the trail a little way to experience the change in the forest as you gain elevation. You will also get a good view from several overlooks back into the gorge you just hiked.

One summer day, while hiking along the upper end of this trail, we stopped in a grassy clearing for lunch. After eating, we stretched out on the grass for an early afternoon snooze. A few minutes after getting comfortable, we heard what we thought was a horse coming up the trail.

The horse stopped, but both of us were too comfortable to be bothered, so we just ignored it. Another minute or two passed. Out of curiosity we opened our eyes to see why the horse had stopped.

Across the clearing, less than twenty yards away, stood an unbelievably large deer. We both had seen deer in the Smokies for years, but nothing to match the size of this magnificent creature.

The deer was wary. He remained just inside the clearing, standing nearly motionless for the better part of fifteen minutes. Occasionally he would turn his head, displaying a noble rack of antlers. He had intuitively detected our presence but was unable to confirm to his satisfaction that all was safe. Finally, just as cool and confidently as he had strode up the trail, he turned and descended the way he had come. He was well into the woods before the light gallop of his hooves could no longer be heard.

How far you choose to hike up Gunter Fork Trail is optional. The farther you hike, the more change in vegetation you will see. When you have seen enough, just re-trace your route back to the trailhead. We recommend that you turn and retrace your steps about half an hour beyond the water slide. 🚶🚶

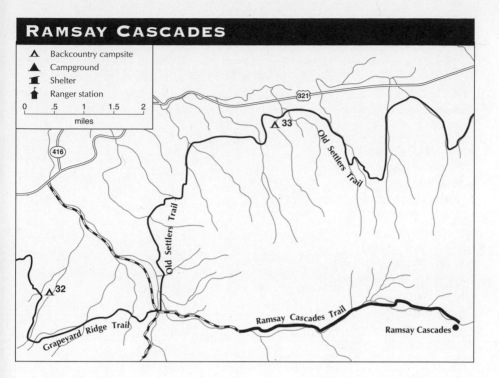

RAMSAY CASCADES

Distance: 8.0 miles round-trip.

Elevation gain: 2,300 feet.

Brief trail description: The trail to Ramsay Cascades is fairly easy for most of its course. As it nears the cascades, the trail climbs through tiers of rock that flank the stream. The rocky surfaces adjacent to the cascades are slick and can be hazardous, as they are continuously moistened by the splashing from the falls.

How to get there: Drive along US 321 to the Greenbrier access 5.9 miles east of Gatlinburg. Turn south (right) onto the paved Greenbrier Cove Road following the Little Pigeon River into Greenbrier Cove. The road's surface changes to gravel shortly before reaching a junction with the Ramsay Prong Road at 3.2 miles. Turn left at the junction and cross the bridge over the river onto the Ramsay Prong Road. The road is blocked 1.5 miles above the junction. The Ramsay Cascades Trail begins at the blocked road.

0.0—Ramsay Prong Road (parking area).

1.5—Road turnaround.

4.0—Ramsay Cascades.

 Ramsay Cascades is unequivocally the most spectacular waterfall in the Smokies. It lies deep in the heart of an ancient, undisturbed forest, where Ramsay Prong plunges violently over a rocky edifice before spilling down a rugged rock face. The waterfall marks the upper terminus of the Ramsay Cascades Trail, six miles above Greenbrier Cove.

The drive into Greenbrier Cove along the Middle Prong of the Little Pigeon River is one of the more picturesque excursions in the Smokies. The trail begins along the stream at the parking area that marks the end of the Ramsay Prong Road. The first one and a half miles of the trail follows a disused segment of the Ramsay Prong Road which traces the course of the Middle Prong of the Little Pigeon River.

Early one May, while hiking along this stretch of road, we were literally surrounded by thousands of yellow butterflies and felt rather like extras in the opening scene from Disney's *Song of the South*. The road follows the course of the stream to its confluence with Ramsay Prong at the base of the Guyot Spur. Here the road ends in a turnaround and the trail to Ramsay Cascades eases onto a footpath and angles into the crease between Pinnacle Lead and Guyot Spur, a long hollow that channels Ramsay Prong.

Ramsay Prong flows through one of the finest primitive wilderness areas in the Smokies. The trail along the stream is lined with large chestnut oaks, silverbells, yellow poplars, black cherry trees, hemlocks, and yellow birches. The high canopy and the rushing stream make this a refreshingly cool hike on a hot day and an ideal environment for ferns, mosses, lichens, and other mountain flora.

Exceptionally large chestnut oaks are found on the lower stretch, while near record-size yellow poplars and black cherries adorn the upper portion. Look around as you hike and notice the small saplings growing on top of the trunks of fallen trees. These are yellow birches and will eventually send their roots around the host log and to the ground. When the host log eventually rots away, the mature seedling will be left standing on it roots.

Frequently while hiking this trail you will hear the jungle-like call of the pileated woodpecker, the largest of the many domestic woodpeckers. Pileated (pronounced like "PIE Lee ate it") is from a Latin word, *pileus,* meaning cap. While all woodpeckers have some red on their heads, no other species can compare to the bright red head on this large, crow-sized, black bird with white speckles on the feathers. Like all woodpeckers, this bird is a tree climber who is generally seen hanging on the trunk of a tree, cocking its head from side to side listening for insects under the bark.

There are also many good examples of "imprisoned rocks" along this trail. This occurs when trees sprout and grow atop boulders and the tree roots gradually surround the boulder in a kind of bear hug. Birch trees are notorious for this stretching of their roots around rocks in this manner.

At one and a half miles above the turnaround, the trail crosses a footlog from the Pinnacle Lead side of Ramsay Prong to the Guyot Spur Side. At this point the

Ramsay Cascades.
Courtesy of Great Smoky
Mountains National Park.

forest takes on a more primordial look and the trees increase noticeably in size. Shortly after the crossing, the trail passes through a stand of cucumber trees, which are adorned by bright, canary-yellow blossoms in the spring. Just before the trail switches back to the Pinnacle Lead side, the undergrowth disappears and the trail passes through the Cherry Orchard, a grove of large black cherry trees, buckeyes, red maples, tulip poplars, and hemlocks.

Just before reaching the cascades, the trail winds its way up through large rough boulders. The progression is more of a stair-stepping exercise than actual rock climbing, but it provides a suitable prelude to the ruggedness of the waterfall and its boulder-strewn environs.

At Ramsay Cascades, two strong streamlets rush over a stratified ledge, then pummel over a series of smaller ledges that line a rock face more than eighty feet high. The effect in bright sunlight is particularly dramatic. There are eight or more distinct plunges where the water cascades over the ledges and into a deep pool at the base of the falls. Here the stream rests momentarily before dashing off and continuing its course to Greenbrier Cove.

There are several fine spots among the rocks for spreading, and devouring, a well-earned lunch. The cascades and rushing water act as giant air conditioners on hot summer days. Even on the hottest days, a long stop near the pool will thoroughly chill the average hiker. The hike back is along the same route, and the moderate downhill grade makes it seem much shorter than the inbound hike. 𝕏

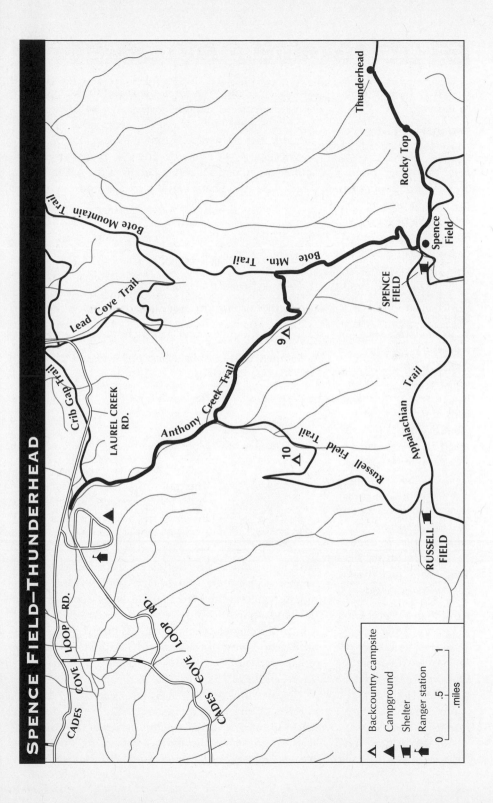

SPENCE FIELD–THUNDERHEAD

Thunderhead

Rocky Top

Spence Field

SPENCE FIELD

Bote Mtn. Trail

Bote Mountain Trail

Lead Cove Trail

Crib Gap Trail

LAUREL CREEK RD.

Anthony Creek Trail

△9

△10

Russell Field Trail

Appalachian Trail

RUSSELL FIELD

CADES COVE LOOP RD.

CADES COVE LOOP RD.

△ Backcountry campsite
▲ Campground
🏠 Shelter
🏠 Ranger station

0   .5   1
.miles

SPENCE FIELD–THUNDERHEAD

Distance: 14.4 miles round-trip.

Elevation gain: 3,565 feet.

Brief trail description: Thunderhead Mountain, the highest peak in the western Smokies, and Spence Field, the largest grassy bald in the Park, lie cheek by jowl along the stateline divide. The most popular approach to the Spence Field–Thunderhead Mountain area follows the Anthony Creek Trail from the upper end of Cades Cove. Its course is long and fairly steep, and somewhat difficult to hike. To reach Thunderhead Mountain from Spence Field requires climbing another fairly steep mile. Hikers with sufficient time and extra stamina may wish to return to Cades Cove via the Russell Field Trail, about three miles east of Spence Field.

How to get there: Enter the Park at Townsend, Tennessee, and drive one mile to the Townsend Wye, where the Little River Road intersects Laurel Creek Road. Or, from the Sugarlands Visitor Center drive the Little River Road 20 miles to the Townsend Wye. Enter the Laurel Creek Road and continue 7 miles to Cades Cove. Just prior to reaching Cades Cove, turn left toward the Cades Cove Campground, then immediately turn left again into the Cades Cove Picnic Grounds. The trail to Spence Field and Thunderhead Mountain begins at the Anthony Creek Trail at the back of the picnic grounds.

0.0—Cades Cove Picnic Grounds (parking area).

0.2—Crib Gap Trail leads left.

1.7—Russell Field Trail leads right.

2.9—Anthony Creek Backcountry Campsite.

3.6—Bote Mountain Trail leads right to Spence Field.

5.4—Spence Field. Appalachian trail leads left to Thunderhead Mountain.

5.8—Jenkins Ridge Trail leads right.

6.5—Rocky Top.

7.2—Thunderhead Mountain.

 The trail to Spence Field and Thunderhead Mountain begins along the lower terminus of the Anthony Creek Trail near the upper end of the Cades Cove Picnic Grounds. This route, one of the shortest to Spence Field, follows a streamside course for the first two miles before entering a steep climb up the flank of Bote Mountain. The lowland along Anthony Creek, once occupied by a grist mill and a cluster of small farms, is now recovered to a fine second-growth poplar forest. In April and May, this area is particularly good for wildflowers, especially trilliums and dwarf irises.

The first mile of the trail is a level jeep track with firm footing. A quarter of a mile above the picnic grounds, the trail intersects the upper terminus of the Crib Gap Trail, then passes through a horse camp. Along Anthony Creek there are five stream crossings, each with its own unique view up and down this picturesque mountain stream. All are adorned with either a bridge or a footlog with a hand rail.

As the trail climbs Bote Mountain the surrounding forest makes a gradual transition from hemlock and rhododendron to a predominately cove hardwood association. After a mile, the trail becomes steeper and rockier. About one and a half miles above the picnic grounds, the Left Prong merges into Anthony Creek near a fine grove of large poplars. Here, the lower terminus of the Russell Field Trail intersects from the right. For the hiker with sufficient time, the Russell Field offers an attractive alternate route for returning from Spence Field.

A half-mile above this junction the Anthony Creek Trail makes a final stream crossing and re-enters the cove hardwood forest where it narrows as it rises above the stream. The occasional deposits of horse dung along the trail keep hikers alert and provide an interesting "wildlife" experience. There would be a lot more manure on the horse trails if it were not for the tireless efforts of the dung beetles. These thumb-nail-size black-shelled insects roll the dung into perfect balls and remove them from the trail for use as a food source.

Within another half-mile, the trail enters a grove of large hemlock trees harboring the Anthony Creek Back Country Campsite. Just above the campsite the trail turns hard to the left and begins a steep ascent of Bote Mountain. The climb is strenuous, but the effort is rewarded by occasional glimpses into the deep-green distant fields of Cades Cove nestled among surrounding ridges.

At the crest of Bote Mountain, the Anthony Creek Trail terminates into a wide jeep

View across Spence Field to Thunderhead Mountain. Courtesy of Great Smoky Mountains National Park.

track known as the Bote Mountain Trail. This trail was once part of the Anderson Road, which ran from Schoolhouse Gap on Scott Mountain at the Park boundary to Spence Field. The road was built by Cherokee workers under the guidance of Reverend Isaac Anderson. Before beginning the project, Anderson consulted the Cherokees as to whether the road should follow the long ridge just east of Cades Cove or another ridge further to the east. The Cherokees "voted" on the two routes and, since their language has no sound for the letter *v*, the closest being *b*, they "boted" for the nearer route, hence the name Bote Mountain. The other ridge was subsequently named Defeat Ridge.

About a third of a mile above the intersection, the jeep track terminates at a circular turnaround where a narrower, rougher trail continues on to Spence Field. Just below Spence Field, the trail passes a large spring, then curls up and into the bald to intersect with the Appalachian Trail.

Spence Field is a grassy bald of several acres spanning the Tennessee–North Carolina border. The bald is named for James Spence, who built a summer cabin here for his family in the 1830s. Spence almost certainly enlarged whatever bald existed here when he arrived.

A few yards to the right of the upper terminus of the Bote Mountain Trail, the Appalachian Trail intersects the upper terminus of the Eagle Creek Trail. The Eagle Creek Trail leads across Spence Field four hundred yards to the Spence Field Shelter. The shelter sits on the site of the old Spence Cabin, where a man named Uncle Tom Sparks was murdered in 1926 in a fight over liquor. Alcohol was undoubtedly a very valuable commodity when you consider what a trip to the store from this remote mountaintop would entail.

To reach Thunderhead Mountain, proceed east (left) along the Appalachian Trail across Spence Field. At the east end of the field, the Appalachian Trail is intersected by the upper terminus of the Jenkins Ridge Trail leading in from North Carolina. A hundred yards or so downhill from this junction lies a fine spring, and near it there once stood a six-person backcountry shelter.

Several years ago one of the authors encountered a large bear behind this shelter. The bear was not friendly.

> Unlike the vast majority of the bears I had encountered in the Smokies, this fellow did not flee into the woods. Instead, he stood and stared at me. Presently he started making a low groaning sound which became increasing louder. The bear then raised his head slightly and made his ears lay back. The groaning sound quickly degenerated into a deep "woof" at which point the bear charged.
>
> I turned and ran. Fortunately for me, the bear's action was only a bluff and he aborted his charge after advancing only a few yards.

From the Jenkins Ridge junction the Appalachian Trail climbs to the top of Thunderhead Mountain. Before reaching Thunderhead, the trail runs through a "mini-bald" adorned with scores of bleached-out rocks. This is Rocky Top, presumably the inspiration for the University of Tennessee's fight song of that name. From here, there is a clear view of Spence Field to the west and, to the south, of Blockhouse Mountain, with its endless backdrop of mountains and ridges.

Stunted and gnarled beech trees stand guard over the last quarter-mile of ridge leading to Thunderhead. During the last century, Thunderhead was a bald, kept clear by cattle and sheep grazing on the rich grass. The pasture has since been overrun with countless weather-beaten rhododendron. A pile of rocks on the summit of the mountain provides a vantage point for looking over the vegetation and enjoying a 360-degree view of mountain terrain.

And what a view it is. Endless foliage-covered peaks, ridges, and valleys. To the east stands Clingmans Dome, the highest peak in the Smokies, and to the left of the Dome is Mount Le Conte. If the air is exceptionally clear, Knoxville, Maryville, and Fort Loudoun Lake will be visible beyond Chilhowee Range to the north.

To the west, the blue Fontana Lake lies in stark contrast to the unending sea of green in every other direction. Far beyond Spence Field lies Gregory Bald, and down below are the emerald fields of Cades Cove.

To the south lie endless layers of mountain ranges. They were formed from a great plain that had been uplifted by a continental plate pushing beneath it to the northwest. The forces of nature then eroded the plain to form what we now see as mountains. Looking at the layer upon layer extending as far as the eye can see, it is easy to imagine the streams, rivers, and winds that worked tirelessly for over 250 million years to carve them.

At this point the Appalachian Trail continues north to Maine, but you will reverse course back through Spence Field. The trip back, however, will seem like a new hike. No matter how many times you look over your shoulder coming up, there is still a fresh look and feel to this trail on the way down. Rather than returning via the Bote Mountain Trail, you may want to continue west along the Appalachian Trail and use the Russell Field Trail for your descent back into Cades Cove. This route will add about three miles to the hike.

Some of the finest open hardwoods in these mountains stand along the two and a half miles between Spence and Russell Fields. In the late spring the floor of this forest will be covered with a variety of wildflowers. The grade is easy on the hiker and passes by Mount Squires and through Little Bald, with yet another view of Fontana Lake. This is also a prime area for grouse, one of the largest game birds in these mountains.

We were hiking through here one fall when a particularly large grouse, who had roosted in the camouflaging grass along the trail, decided to wait until we were right beside him to take flight. Whenever surprised, grouse make a loud fluttering sound and dart from their cover. When you are out in the wilderness and you hear something that loud, that close, your first thought is "a bear!" Once your heartbeat returns to normal, you feel a little foolish when you realize it was actually only a bird.

We came upon an old-time mountaineer on one hike who told us about a wonderful survival strategy adopted by baby grouse. Whenever a mother and her chicks are surprised, the mother goes into a fluttering crawl to distract the potential enemy. The chicks, meanwhile, each grab a dead leaf in their beak and roll downhill into a pile of dead leaves. They lay there beneath their camouflage until the coast is clear.

After another mile, the trail rises into Russell Field, a pleasant mountain clearing in the fork of two ridges flanking Russell Field Branch. Russell Field harbors a shelter supplied by a spring fifty yards down the trail on the Tennessee side. Indians probably used this location as a hunting camp before it was settled by farmers and herders. In the latter part of the nineteenth century, barns and cabins stood at this location.

A friendly little three-legged skunk used to inhabit the edge of the woods here. Not unlike Blanche DuBois in *A Streetcar Named Desire,* he depended on the kindness of strangers and, judging from his plump physique, strangers in these parts are generous indeed. If he should approach you for a handout, he would sell his soul for dried pineapple.

The Appalachian Trail continues on to the west, while Russell Field Trail runs down the mountain to the right. It exits north along the back of the hollow above the spring to begin a gradual descent to Russell Field Branch. About a mile and a quarter from the shelter you will leave the boggy field and start down a drier stretch lined with rhododendron, hardwoods, and pines.

A brief, but easy, descent about halfway down will signal the beginning of a rocky and wet stretch of trail through some of the oldest trees remaining on this end of the park. Horses and rain, combined with the steep terrain, make this a potential ankle-turner for the weary hiker. There are big trees to draw one's attention, so "slow and steady" is good advice for this interval.

Almost three miles from the top the trail passes a campsite, which means there is only three-quarters of a mile of easy downhill hiking before the trail rejoins Anthony Creek Trail. Just beyond the campsite the trail fords Left Prong at a spot that will require some tricky rock hopping on slippery rocks and logs. It is often easier to just remove your footgear and wade the narrow stream rather than finish the hike with wet boots or a sprained ankle. There will be a second crossing, this time on a footlog, hard on the heels of the first. The trail continues through some truly impressive old-growth hemlocks before ending at Anthony Creek Trail. A left turn and retracing one and a half miles of your initial hike will end at the Cades Cove parking lot. 🚶

CLINGMANS DOME–SILERS BALD

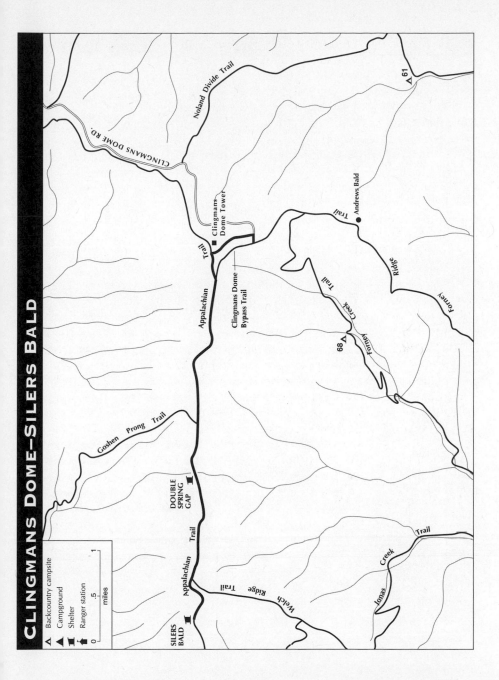

Legend:
- △ Backcountry campsite
- ▲ Campground
- ⛫ Shelter
- ⛿ Ranger station

0   .5   1
miles

CLINGMANS DOME RD.

Noland Divide Trail

Clingmans Dome Tower

Clingmans Dome Bypass Trail

Appalachian Trail

Andrews Bald

Forney Ridge Trail

Forney Creek Trail

△ 68

△ 61

Goshen Prong Trail

DOUBLE SPRING GAP

Appalachian Trail

SILERS BALD

Welch Ridge Trail

Jonas Creek Trail

Distance: 10.0 miles round-trip.

Elevation loss: 1,040 feet.

Brief trail description: This course follows the Appalachian Trail from Clingmans Dome, the highest point in the Smokies, to Silers Bald, a highland grassy bald once grazed by livestock. Clingmans Dome sports a 45-foot observation tower that affords an exceptionally fine 360-degree panoramic view of the greater Smoky Mountain environs. The view from Silers Bald is less spectacular and limited mainly to the Tennessee side. The trail between the two peaks is rugged underfoot in several places but is not strenuous going from east to west. The return from Silers Bald to Clingmans Dome, however, is rather steep where the trail ascends Mount Buckley immediately west of Clingmans Dome.

How to get there: The trailhead lies along the edge of the Clingmans Dome parking lot at the upper end of the 7-mile Clingmans Dome Road. The Clingmans Dome Road (closed in winter) begins in Newfound Gap, where the Newfound Gap Road (US 441) crosses over the stateline divide. Newfound Gap is about 13 miles southeast of the Sugarland Visitor Center, near Gatlinburg, and about 15 miles northwest of the Oconaluftee Visitor Center, near Cherokee, North Carolina.

0.0—Clingmans Dome Road (parking area).

0.5—Clingmans Dome Tower.

0.7—Clingmans Dome Bypass Trail leads left.

2.7—Goshen Prong Trail leads right.

3.3—Double Spring Gap Shelter.

4.3—The Narrows.

4.6—Welch Ridge Trail leads left.

4.8—Silers Bald.

5.0—Silers Bald Shelter.

No one knows for certain where the name "Great Smoky Mountains" originated or how it gained prominence in the mountain vernacular. It was perhaps an adaptation of the name "Smoky Dome," a moniker applied by the earliest white settlers to the peak now known as Clingmans Dome. The dome, like most of the higher peaks in the mountains, is often shrouded by a tenuous blue mist which readily suggests the source of the name.

When white settlers first began arriving in the Smokies, Clingmans Dome was virtually inaccessible. It was high and remote, and covered by impenetrable stands of closely growing Fraser firs. Today the summit of the dome is capped with a concrete observation tower reached by a handicapped-accessible ramp. A paved pathway approaches the tower, leading up from the Clingmans Dome parking area a little under three-quarters of a mile below the summit.

On a clear day the tower provides a unique panoramic view up and down the spine of the Great Smoky Mountains. The most prominent vertebrae along this east-west axis are Mounts Cammerer, Guyot, Chapman, Kephart, Silers Bald, and Thunderhead. There are orientation plaques affixed to the tower identifying the landmarks visible from the dome. North of the stateline divide, Mount Le Conte is the most prominent peak, rising majestically beyond the Sugarlands valley. To the south, an endless series of ramifying ridges, layer upon layer, roll deep into western North Carolina.

To begin the hike to Silers Bald, follow the short path from the base of the tower to the Appalachian Trail. The initial part of the course follows through a rich boreal forest where dark and closely set balsams rise above a spongy humus floor of decaying flora.

On leaving Clingmans Dome, the trail begins negotiating the jagged edges of upturned rock strata along the spine of the divide. The Appalachian Trail, in addition to being well graded and easy to follow, is marked with white paint blazes on the trees and rocks along the path. Numerous rock ramparts along this stretch protrude over the adjacent valley, affording breathtaking overlooks into the Tennessee side.

About a half-mile beyond the dome, the trail begins a long, steep descent down Mount Buckley, the ragged western shoulder of Clingmans Dome. Here the dark green ranks of the balsams gradually yield to the lighter hardwoods which dominate the western end of the Smokies. The trail descends through alternating stands of balsams, semi-balds, and groves of beeches, buckeyes, and Allegheny serviceberries.

The intersection with the Goshen Prong Trail heralds the long easy approach to Double Springs Gap, a small opening in the beech belt that harbors two fine springs and the Double Spring Shelter. A few years ago there were two deer, a doe and a buck, who spent virtually the entire summer lurking around this shelter. They had obviously been tamed by illegal handouts from the numerous hikers passing by or stopping for the night. Hikers had named the buck Rhett and the doe, Scarlet.

The springs in this clearing are on opposite sides of the stateline divide. Although they are only fifty yards apart, the waters flow hundreds of miles through two different states before mingling again at the confluence of the Tennessee and Little Tennessee Rivers. The small North Carolina spring flows into a convenient rock basin while the more prolific Tennessee spring fans out into an exceedingly messy bog.

Especially in the spring and fall, you may run into "through-hikers" along this stretch of the Appalachian Trail. In the spring the northbound folks will be striding purposefully through on their way to Maine. In the fall, the southbound troops will be marching toward the finish line in Georgia. These intrepid backpackers are a breed unto themselves. They hike the entire trail in one summer, subsisting mainly on oatmeal, macaroni and cheese, and peanut butter.

We always bring extra fresh fruit when we stay in one of the shelters on the Appalachian Trail in the hopes of running into one of these nomads. We once gave an orange to a through hiker who hadn't had any fresh food at all for over three weeks. He ate half and asked if we would mind if he saved the other half for breakfast. Old softies that we are, we broke down and gave him an apple as well. Take some fruit to share and, if you encounter a through-hiker, you might make a friend for life.

West of Double Springs, the trail cuts through some of the healthiest stands of Allegheny serviceberry trees in these mountains. In the spring the slopes are covered with a pinkish-white blanket of spring beauties shaded by the pale pink serviceberry blossoms. Along here the forest is conveniently broken by grassy semi-balds which afford panoramic views of the distant slopes of western North Carolina and the upper embayments of Fontana Lake. Occasionally hikers along this section of the trail may notice large patches of freshly upturned sod, cut as though it had been worked haphazardly by a garden hoe. These disturbed places are the work of wild boars rooting for the corms of flowering herbs.

One spring, when the slopes along the trail above Double Spring Gap were festooned with blossoming wildflowers, one of the authors was hiking alone through this section. Having become tired, he decided to take a short nap and wandered off the trail on the North Carolina side in search of a suitable spot. About three hundred yards from the trail he stopped and stretched out on the ground at the top of a slight rise. After a few minutes under the influence of the warm sun, he was asleep.

I was awakened from my light slumber by the sound of grass being ripped from the ground. I opened by eyes and turned my head toward the sound. Less than twenty feet away stood the biggest wild boar I had ever seen, standing completely motionless and staring directly at me. His snout was down to the ground and two long, ivory-colored tusks protruded menacingly from his lower jaw. Nary a bristle stirred nor a muscle twitched.

This was clearly more than just another occasion in my hiking experience where I was at a complete loss. I could foresee no way of extracting myself from the apparent danger. A quick mental review of my pathetically limited knowledge of boars proved useless. However, I remembered reading somewhere that boars were fast and unpredictable; I quickly surmised that one wrong move on my part might likely provoke a charge. I remained calmly terrified, watching the red glint in his eye for any clue to his disposition.

After a sustained period of absolute stillness, the beast moved his head slightly to one side, still training his eye firmly on me. After an infinite pause, he moved in a manner I would never have anticipated. He turned completely around and faced me straight on.

I glanced around for a tree suitable to climb in the event the beast charged. Presently, however, he turned and trotted a few steps down the rise, then stopped and turned back. Again he trotted a few steps, then stopped and looked back again as though he were undecided about what to do.

Finally the boar began working his way up the adjacent ridge, stopping every few feet to contemplate his course of action. He eventually retreated over the ridge and out of sight.

About halfway between Double Spring Gap and Silers Bald, the trail cuts abruptly to the right to clear a white quartz outcropping that straddles the ridgeline. Here the trail enters the Narrows, a rocky, razor-edge where the harrowing winds of winter roar up from the deep hollows below. The journey through the Narrows terminates just prior to the trail's intersection with the Welch Ridge Trail, near the base of Silers Bald. A steep, but mercifully brief, climb leads to the summit of Silers, which is marked by a small, rounded boulder bearing a U.S. Geological Survey medallion.

A short path leads north from the summit of the bald to a rock rampart that offers a fine view into the Little River drainage and across to Cove Mountain. This is the only vantage point from Silers as the bald has been largely overtaken by the resurging forest.

The Silers Bald Shelter is located on the west end of the bald. While staying in the shelter a few summers ago, we were visited by a skunk intent on getting a handout. The skunk busied himself checking into everything while we were trying to fix our supper. To distract the little critter, we placed a garbage bag out on the ground away from the shelter in hopes that he would be enticed to it.

The ploy worked. The skunk climbed into the bag and began happily rummaging around for whatever delectable morsels the garbage afforded. The skunk had been at work for only a few minutes when a bear approached. Not needing a bear-skunk fight in our camp, we desperately tried to scare off the bear and coax the skunk out the bag. The bear was an experienced panhandler and was not deterred by our shouting and waving. The skunk, likewise, was not to be denied.

Our only recourse was rash action. It was decided that someone should dash out, quickly close the mouth of the bag, then toss the bag, skunk and all, into the woods away from the camp. This initiative required a manly man, and that, we lacked.

Fortunately for us, the bear knew skunks. When he discovered the little fellow buried in the bag, he very quickly retreated and disappeared into the woods.

While the skunk feasted, we busied ourselves plugging up all the holes under the fence enclosing the shelter, using logs, rocks, and pieces of discarded boards and sheet metal. When the skunk finished with the garbage, he couldn't get back into the shelter. We congratulated ourselves on a job well done, finished supper, and went to bed.

We had been asleep about an hour when the skunk returned, rattling the sheet metal, clacking rocks, and pulling at the wire fence in an attempt to dislodge the obstruction. For the better part of the next two hours, the little varmint kept banging and rattling, keeping everyone awake. Finally a voice rang out, "He's in." He went quietly to some old garbage in the fireplace, and we finally got to sleep.

A little later we were awakened by another voice in the dark, "He's up on the bunks." Then another spoke out, "He just climbed over my feet." A minute later, another voice, "He just crawled over my face." Those on the top tier of bunks roared with laughter.

Next, we heard the metallic ring of a stainless steel pot lid hitting the wooden bunk. The skunk had gotten into our freshly boiled, bacteria-free water that we had set out to cool for the next day's hike. We were soon lulled to sleep by the gentle rhythm of the skunk's lap-lap-lapping of the water.

The hike from Silers Bald back to Clingmans Dome entails a steep climb up Mount Buckley. The trail on Mount Buckley is well graded and the scenery exceptionally pleasant, and thus one does not necessarily notice the steepness while descending from Clingmans Dome. However, at the end of a long day, the hike back up Mount Buckley can be quite strenuous and exhausting. 🏃🏃

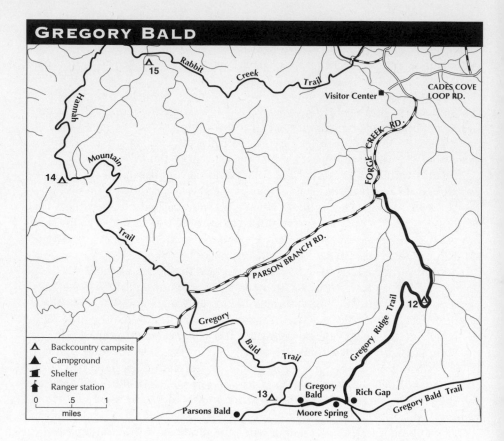

GREGORY BALD

Rabbit Creek Trail

△ 15

Hannah

Mountain

14 △

Trail

Visitor Center ■

CADES COVE
LOOP RD.

FORGE CREEK RD.

PARSON BRANCH RD.

Gregory

Bald

Trail

Gregory Ridge Trail

12 △

△ Backcountry campsite
▲ Campground
🏠 Shelter
👤 Ranger station

0   .5   1
        miles

13 △

Gregory
Bald

Rich Gap

Gregory Bald Trail

Parsons Bald ●

Moore Spring ●

Distance: 11.6 miles round-trip.

Elevation gain: 3,020 feet.

Brief trail description: Gregory Bald is a large, highland meadow that straddles the stateline divide near the western end of the Smokies. The bald has always been one of the finest vantage points in the mountains and is especially noted for its exceptional views of the beautiful Cades Cove basin. More recently, the bald has become recognized for its brilliant mid-June displays of flame azaleas. Gregory Bald can be reached from many directions, but the most popular and most accessible is the Gregory Ridge Trail route originating from the southwest corner of Cades Cove. This trail has an elevation gain of over 2,500 feet and will take the average hiker four hours to reach the bald.

How to get there: Enter the Park at Townsend, Tennessee, and drive one mile to the Townsend Wye, where the Little River Road intersects Laurel Creek Road. Or, from the Sugarlands Visitor Center, drive the Little River Road 18.8 miles to the Townsend Wye. Then drive along Laurel Creek Road 7.0 miles to Cades Cove and enter the Cades Cove Loop Road. Continue the Cades Cove Loop Road 4.0 miles to Cables Mill at the southwest corner of the cove. Here the entrance to Cables Mill turns right and the Cades Cove Loop Road turns left. Straight ahead, the gravel Forge Creek Road leads 2 miles to terminate in a turnaround. The Gregory Ridge Trail begins along the upper edge of the turnaround.

0.0—Forge Creek Road (parking area).

1.4—Manway to Ekaneetlee Gap.

2.0—Forge Creek Backcountry Campsite.

5.0—Rich Gap. Gregory Bald Trail leads right to Gregory Bald.

5.6—Manway leads left 200 yards to Moore Spring.

5.8—Gregory Bald.

The Gregory Ridge Trail begins along the upper end of a turnaround near a former homesite at the junction of Forge Creek Road and Parsons Branch Road. On leaving the turnaround, the Gregory Ridge Trail follows Forge Creek upstream through a cluster of abandoned farm fields and into a forest of tulip poplar trees five or six feet in diameter that rise straight as shipmasts for seventy-five feet without a branch before bursting out in a great green canopy high over the trail.

About one and a half miles above the turnaround and near the junction of Ekaneetlee Branch and Forge Creek, the trail passes the rotting remains of a huge, fallen poplar tree, once known as Big Poplar. This tree was among the largest in the Smokies and was often cited as a landmark identifying the head of an ancient Cherokee trace that crossed over the mountain at Ekaneetlee Gap on the stateline divide and descended into North Carolina.

Two miles above the turnaround, the trail leaves the stream and circles around the Forge Creek Backcountry Campsite, then begins a moderate, but steady, three-mile climb up and along Gregory Ridge to the stateline divide at Rich Gap. Several years ago, when cattle still grazed the highland fields of the Smoky Mountains, Rich Gap was a clearing occupied by a "gant" lot. According to chronicler Horace Kephart, a gant lot was "a fenced enclosure into which cattle are driven after cutting them out from those of other owners. So called because the mountain cattle run wild, feeding only on grass and browse, and 'they couldn't travel well to market when filled up on green stuff; so they're penned up to get *gant* and nimble.'"

At Rich Gap, the Gregory Ridge Trail intersects the Gregory Bald Trail following along the spine of the stateline divide. Gregory Bald lies to the right (west) along the Gregory Bald Trail about a half-mile above Rich Gap. The trail to the bald is a moderate grade through a sparse forest which is gradually reclaiming the grassy fields that once occupied the ridgeline.

Gregory Bald is a ten-acre, dome-shaped clearing which sits astride the Tennessee–North Carolina border. It was once prized by cattle farmers as a rich upland grazing range. Members of several notable Cades Cove families herded at Gregory Bald. Russell Gregory was the first to build a cabin on the bald. His cabin was a cylindrical, stone structure with large windows which he called "portholes." In the evening, Gregory would poke his rife, "Old Long Tom," through one of the "portholes" and shoot deer that approached to lick salt set out for the cattle.

Although salt licks are no longer set out on Gregory Bald, deer still return every evening. One warm April afternoon, one of the authors was stretched out comfortably on the thick grass that covers the bald, taking a well-earned nap. "While I was sleeping, a small doe crept up and, apparently mistaking my head for a block of salt, licked me squarely between the eyes. Although I yelped and jumped up quickly to confront the intruder, the deer seemed totally unperturbed, apparently quite accustomed to licking sweaty hikers for her daily supplement of salt."

The deer on Gregory are more forward than their compatriots from other areas of the Park. A few years ago we hiked up for a gourmet picnic while the azaleas were at their peaks. We gathered around some non-traditional picnic fare that included lemon chicken, sesame noodles, and white chocolate macadamia nut cookies. A large doe watching from the edge of the woods strode gingerly up to our ground cloth and, after inspecting the fare, gingerly plucked a loaf of homemade walnut bread from a nearby basket.

There is long-standing speculation that Gregory is a natural bald. William Davenport, an early explorer who charted the main crest of the Smokies in the 1820s, recorded seeing two "bald spots" in this vicinity of the Smokies. The description and proximity of the "bald spots" suggests that Davenport was referring to Gregory and the nearby Parsons Bald.

In Davenport's day, Gregory Bald was much larger, the view more open, and the atmosphere clearer than now. Accounts by early visitors suggest that as many as five states could be seen from the bald. Then, all of Cades Cove was visible as well as Happy Valley and the windings of the Little Tennessee River.

More recently Gregory Bald has become famed for its brilliant mid-June displays of flame azaleas. Fifty years ago, Harvey Broome described the azaleas on Gregory as being "of diverse hues, running from pure white through all the pinks, yellows, salmons, and flames, to deep saturated reds" and "ranged in such delightfully un-studied stands around the edge it seemed as though it had all been done by design." In the fifty years that have transpired, the bald has undergone changes. The forests have surged back, overleaping the azaleas and spotting the bald with trees. Tough, low shrubbery has invaded the former expanse of grassy turf. Nevertheless, the aza-leas are still outstanding and Gregory Bald still affords the finest vantage point in the Smokies for an all-encompassing view of the Cades Cove basin. 🚶‍♂️

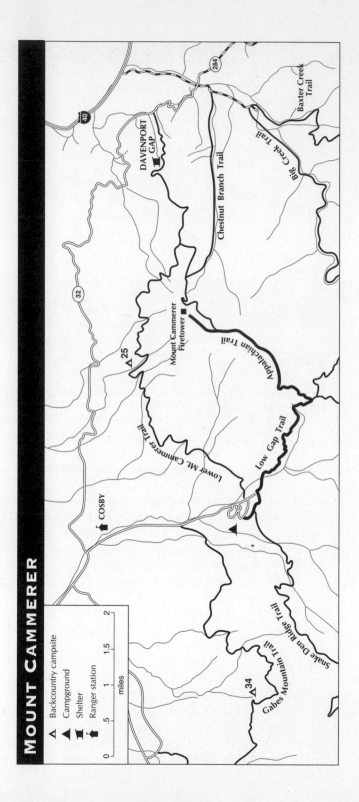

MOUNT CAMMERER

△ Backcountry campsite
▲ Campground
⛺ Shelter
🏠 Ranger station

0   .5   1   1.5   2
miles

COSBY

DAVENPORT GAP

40

284

Baxter Creek Trail

Big Creek Trail

Chestnut Branch Trail

Mount Cammerer Firetower

△ 25

32

Appalachian Trail

Low Gap Trail

Lower Mt. Cammerer Trail

Snake Den Ridge Trail

Gabes Mountain Trail

△ 34

Distance: 10.4 miles round-trip.

Elevation gain: 2,500 feet.

Brief trail description: Mount Cammerer can be reached from Davenport Gap on the TN 32–NC 284 road at the stateline divide, from Walnut Bottom above the Deep Creek Campground, or from the Cosby Campground. The trail from the Cosby Campground is considerably shorter than that from Deep Creek and easier than that from Davenport Gap. From the Cosby Campground, the trail to Mount Cammerer follows first the Low Gap Trail to the stateline divide, then the Appalachian Trail going east. The entire course is well graded and fairly easy to hike but can be strenuous in a few places.

How to get there: From Gatlinburg, drive east on US 321 to TN 32. Turn right and proceed 1.2 miles to the Cosby Cove entrance to the Park. Or, from I-40, drive west to Cosby, then south on TN 32 to Cosby Cove. Turn right into Cosby Cove and drive 2.0 miles to the ranger station. Park here

and walk to the back of the campground. The trail to Mount Cammerer begins on the Low Gap Trail near campsite B99.

0.0—Cosby Campground.

0.3—Utility trail leads right.

0.5—Utility trail leads left.

2.5—Low Gap. Appalachian Trail leads left to Mount Cammerer.

4.6—Spur trail leads left to the Mount Cammerer firetower.

5.2—Mount Cammerer firetower.

Mount Cammerer, a rocky outcropping sitting astride the stateline divide, is the finest vantage point in the northeastern corner of the Smokies. Its summit is capped with an attractive stone firetower built in the fashion of a medieval military outpost. The most popular access to Mount Cammerer begins in the Cosby Campground and follows the Low Gap Trail onto the main divide.

Cosby, once known locally as the Moonshine Capital of the World, is a small, circular basin bounded by the curving stateline divide. The slopes above Cosby are furrowed with rocky, inaccessible hollows, once a bane to the logging operators but a boon to the moonshine industry.

The Low Gap Trail is one of the oldest in the Smokies. Parts of it date back to the earliest white settlements in the mountains when pioneers began moving into Cosby Cove in Tennessee and Walnut Bottom on Big Creek in North Carolina. An important access for settlers, this trail was the only transmountain pass over the main divide east of the old Oconaluftee Turnpike through Indian Gap.

The Low Gap Trail leaves the Cosby Campground along a gravel road, passing a water reservoir and a spur trail that links the Low Gap Trail with the Snake Den Ridge Trail. Five hundred yards above the trailhead, the road terminates in a turnaround. The trail proceeds as a graded path another two hundred yards to cross Cosby Creek on a footlog. On the far side of the creek, another spur exits left a half-mile to a horse concession just west of the campground.

The climb to Low Gap is generally steep and rocky, roughly following the course of Cosby Creek. Along the lower elevations the trail passes through virgin stands of huge hemlocks, buckeyes, and poplars. Higher up, these species diminish and the various species of oak begin to dominate. There is a fine spring beside the trail approximately two miles up, near where the trail crosses Cosby Creek for only the second time. Here, the trail becomes steeper, and soon rises into Low Gap, a V-shaped notch in the stateline divide where it intersects the Appalachian Trail atop the spine of the divide.

Low Gap, predictably, is one of the lowest points along the eastern divide of the Smokies. The gap is spacious, remarkably open, and visible for a short distance as you approach. This is a fairly busy crossroads, where people encounter one another crossing over the mountain.

A curious deer used to keep an eye on this spot. If hikers sat quietly for a few minutes, she would walk out of the woods and begin grazing within a few yards of the hikers. We observed her on two successive years in the same spot. She undoubtedly cleaned up any scraps of food left by hikers.

Firetower on Mount Cammerer. Courtesy of Paul Moore.

The trail to Mount Cammerer leaves east (left) out of Low Gap and ascends steadily along the Appalachian Trail. Two miles above Low Gap, the Appalachian Trail drops off sharply into North Carolina, leaving a spur trail to follow the main ridge another half-mile to Mount Cammerer. Along here, the main crest is a near-vertical layer of slate and rock, narrow on top, with a trough wedged tightly in the fractured ends of the upturned strata. Dense thickets of laurel encumber the entire ridge, pressing the trail into the jagged trough. The trough acts like a receptacle, retaining water and accumulating fallen leaves and other organic detritus which together form a rotting mixture of sticky, black mire.

Old-timers may remember when Mount Cammerer was called White Rock, and those older still may know it as Sharp Top. The name "Sharp Top" probably originated from the slanting, knife-like appearance of the point of the promontory. The cliffs beneath are covered with white, chalky lichen and, from a distance, resemble a large white rock. Inasmuch as White Rock is visible from the valleys below its east end, this name soon displaced "Sharp Top" in local usage. The name was later officially changed to "Mount Cammerer" in tribute to the former director of the National Park Service, Arno B. Cammerer.

Perched atop the prominent outcropping of Mount Cammerer is a squat firetower that resembles a fourteenth-century Norman turret without a castle. The firetower was built according to the "organic style" or the so-called "Yosemite model," a design adapted for rocky outcroppings mainly in the national parks in the western United States. Such towers were rare in the eastern United States, and today only one other of this type, in New Hampshire, still exists.

When completed in the 1930s by the Civilian Conservation Corps, the Mount Cammerer firetower featured a catwalk around its girth and a stone stairway leading to its outer wall. The building fell into disrepair. The catwalk rotted away, the roof was in bad shape, and some of the stone steps were missing. During the spring of 1995, supplies were ferried to Mount Cammerer and the firetower restored to its original condition.

The views from Mount Cammerer are extraordinary. Its promontory extends out high above the eastern end of the mountain range, looking down onto the isolated pocket communities along the deep valley of the Pigeon River, the only stream that cuts through the Appalachian chain between the French Broad and the Little Tennessee River valleys. To the north is Douglas Lake, and beyond, the view is limited only to the extent that the eye fails to distinguish where the blue of the sky and the haze of the mountains fade into the horizon. To the east are the Black and Unaka Mountains, and to the south, the powerful Mount Sterling ridge, readily identified by its prominent firetower.

The majority of hikers return to Cosby Campground along the same route they ascend; however, those with sufficient time and a little extra stamina may wish to return via the Lower Mount Cammerer Trail. This route is a little over five miles longer than the return trip but affords a fine excursion around the rugged eastern shoulder of Mount Cammerer. To take this route, proceed east where the Mount Cammerer spur joins the Appalachian Trail. At this juncture, the Appalachian Trail rolls off the stateline divide and descends steeply along the rocky North Carolina slope. About one mile below Mount Cammerer, the trail passes a fine outcropping overlooking the Pigeon River valley.

About two miles below Mount Cammerer, the Appalachian Trail returns to the stateline divide and intersects the Lower Mount Cammerer Trail in a shallow opening along the ridgeline. The Lower Mount Cammerer Trail circles west around Mount Cammerer and returns to the Cosby Campground near the lower terminus of the Low Gap Trail.

The upper part of the Lower Mount Cammerer Trail follows the contours of the ridges, alternating easily between the dry exposures of the ridge points and the cool, dark recesses of the hollows. The ridges generally bear second-growth, open oak forests while the hollows are often blanketed in wildflowers and usually harbor a tiny stream.

About two miles below its upper terminus, the Lower Mount Cammerer Trail passes the Gilliland Fork Backcountry Campsite. It then works its way around the shoulder of Gilliland Ridge into the deep hollow of the Riding Fork of Caney Creek. In the spring, this area is virtually covered with wildflowers—spring beauties, halberd-leaved yellow violets, bloodroots, wild irises, hepaticas, sweet white violets, and trillium. At the back of the hollow, the trail crosses a long, slender, slow-moving cascade of the Riding Fork.

On leaving the hollow, the trail makes a short climb up and over Sutton Ridge. At the crest of the ridge a spur exits the trail and climbs right two hundred yards to an artificially maintained clearing known as the Sutton Ridge Overlook. From here there are good views into Cosby Cove with Gabes Mountain and Round Mountain providing the immediate background. Directly ahead and beyond the Park boundary is Green Mountain.

The mile and a half that remains is mostly a comfortable walk through a stretch of level forest with a stream crossing of Toms Branch on a footlog followed by another easy creek crossing. The last half-mile of the Lower Mount Cammerer Trail is gravel road, a latter-day improvement of a wagon track that was formerly an integral part of the settlement community at Cosby. Along the road are vestiges of the abandoned settlement, including traces of building plots, stone fences, and a walled-up spring. A few hundred yards from the finish line the trail enters a wide clearing occupied by a horse concession. The road then passes an access spur leading up left from the ranger station on the Cosby Cove access road and quickly fords Cosby Creek before ending at the campground. 🏃

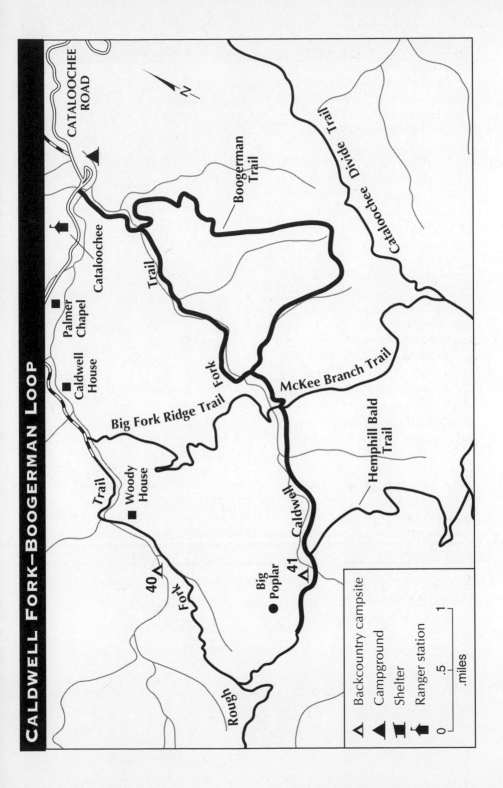

CALDWELL FORK–BOOGERMAN LOOP

CATALOOCHEE ROAD

N

Boogerman Trail

Cataloochee Divide Trail

Cataloochee Trail

Palmer Chapel

Caldwell House

McKee Branch Trail

Big Fork Ridge Trail

Caldwell Fork

Hemphill Bald Trail

Woody House

Caldwell Fork

Trail

40

41

Big Poplar

Rough Fork

Backcountry campsite
Campground
Shelter
Ranger station

0   .5   1
.miles

CALDWELL FORK–BOOGERMAN LOOP

Distance: 12.1 miles round-trip.

Elevation gain: 800 feet.

Brief trail description: The Caldwell Fork–Boogerman loop comprises the lower end of the Caldwell Fork Trail, all of the Boogerman Trail, and part of the upper end of the Caldwell Fork Trail. The Caldwell Fork Trail follows a stream course for three miles before angling off and climbing to its end on Fork Ridge. Boogerman Trail is a half-loop that leaves from and returns to Caldwell Fork Trail. This hike follows Caldwell Fork Trail to Boogerman Trail, then along Boogerman and back to the Caldwell Fork Trail. It then proceeds up Caldwell Fork Trail as far as the Big Poplars, a cluster of large yellow poplar trees. Except for multiple stream crossings along the lower end of the Caldwell Fork Trail, most of this course is fairly easy. The Boogerman portion is nice as it is the only trail in the Cataloochee section free of horse traffic.

How to get there: The entrance to Cataloochee is via old NC 284 (Cove Creek Road) immediately south of exit 20 on I-40. From the south or east, follow US 276 to Dellwood, North Carolina; turn right and continue on US 276. After 5.0 miles, turn left onto Cove Creek Road. This junction is 150 feet before the exit 20 ramp at the I-40 interchange. There is no sign marking Cove Creek Road. After a half-mile along Cove Creek Road, the pavement ends. After another half-mile, a road to Suttontown branches left. The Cove Creek Road continues right, climbing steeply 5.0 miles to the Park boundary at Cove Creek Gap. Cove Creek Road continues through the gap, descending 2.0 miles to Sal Patch Gap and the eastern terminus of the paved Cataloochee Road. To reach Cataloochee, turn left onto the new Cataloochee Road. After descending 3.0 miles, it crosses Cataloochee Creek to intersect the southern terminus of the old Cataloochee Road, a gravel track that leads to the Palmer house and then to old NC 284. One mile beyond this intersection, the new Cataloochee Road passes the Cataloochee Campground with 27 sites for vehicle camping.

0.0—Cataloochee Road (parking area).

0.8—Boogerman Trail leads left.

4.7—Boogerman Trail intersects Caldwell Fork Trail.

5.1—Big Fork Trail leads right.

5.1—McKee Branch Trail leads left.

5.2—Manway leads left to the Shelton-Caldwell gravesite.

5.5—Deadening Fields.

6.6—Hemphill Bald Trail leads left.

6.7—Caldwell Fork Backcountry Campsite.

7.0—Manway leads 100 yards to Big Poplar.

Because of its complicated geography, Cataloochee is one of the least accessible regions in the Smokies. Cataloochee harbors an open meadow that somewhat resembles Cades

Cove on the Tennessee side of the Park. Like Cades Cove, Cataloochee is the flat bottom of a large bowl with high mountains for its sides. Unlike Cades Cove, it is crisscrossed by ridgelines which separate it into two primary coves, Big and Little Cataloochee.

The Cataloochee basin is bounded on the north by Mount Sterling Ridge and on the south by the Cataloochee Divide. Both of these are imposing ridges extending from Balsam Mountain, which encloses the western end of the basin. The eastern end is blocked by the conjunction of White Oak and Scottish Mountains ranging along the Park's boundary. Historically, the most feasible points of entry were Cove Creek Gap and Mount Sterling Gap, situated respectively on the southeastern and northeastern corners of Cataloochee.

Within the basin, the disarray of ridges divides Cataloochee into a complex of coves, the largest of which is Big Cataloochee, a remarkably flat grassland extending along Cataloochee Creek and Rough Fork. Before the arrival of the Park in 1934, Big Cataloochee was farmland and supported an isolated, agrarian community of nearly a thousand people.

Of the nearly two hundred buildings once scattered across this picturesque landscape, only a few remain—the Palmer, Caldwell, and Woody houses; the Will Messer barn; Beech Grove School; and Palmer Chapel. All of these are maintained by the Park Service and, except for the Woody house, can be reached by automobile. With the exception of Cades Cove, Big Cataloochee contains the largest concentration of Appalachian architecture inside the Park.

Two other buildings, the John Jackson Hannah cabin and the Little Cataloochee Baptist Church stand in Little Cataloochee, a sub-cove high under the lee of Mount Sterling and separated from Big Cataloochee by Noland Mountain. Though geographically distinct, blood and marriage joined the two communities. Apple-growing formed the economic base of the tiny hamlet of Ola, the center of the farming settlements clustered in Little Cataloochee.

If time permits, it is well worth an "automobile hike" of the cove as an adjunct to the Caldwell Fork-Boogerman Trail hike.

The Caldwell Fork Trail begins on the left side of the road just above the Cataloochee Campground on a long footlog across Cataloochee Creek. Especially on a sunny day, it is worth stopping halfway across the log to soak up the ambiance of this broad, fast-moving mountain stream.

The trail traces the route of Caldwell Fork as it flows down from its headwaters in Polls Gap into Cataloochee Creek and, like most trails in Cataloochee, doubles as a horse and hiking trail. Look out for some muddy going, especially after a period of rainy weather.

Caldwell Fork carries a latter-day spelling of the Colwell family name. The Colwells, who arrived in the first half of the nineteenth century, were among the first white pioneers to settle in Cataloochee. The first half-mile of the trail runs mostly through groves of pine trees, which makes for some comfortable hiking on the fallen needles. It is a pleasant, if unspectacular, walk.

At a little under a mile, just after passing the confluence of Den Branch and Caldwell Fork, turn left onto the Boogerman Trail. Boogerman is a loop that will rejoin Caldwell Fork Trail further up the stream. We recommend you take Boogerman Trail on the first part of your hike. You will enjoy this unspoiled hike through virgin forest more when you are still fresh.

There are two slightly different versions of how this trail came by its unusual name. The first holds that a teacher once asked young Robert Palmer what he wanted to be when he grew up, and Robert Palmer answered that he wanted to be the booger man.

The second version has the same Robert Palmer, on his very first day of school, being asked by the teacher to give his name. Young Palmer, a shy lad, put his head down on his desk and said the first thing that came to his mind—"Booger Man." The name stuck. From that day forward, Robert Palmer was known as Boogerman or, the more familiar, "Booger."

No matter which version you prefer, one thing is undisputed: his isolationist nature preserved a beautiful corner of the park as virgin forest for future generations. As a young man, Boogerman Palmer sought to escape the crowded Cataloochee valley by building a home in an isolated cove above Caldwell Fork, high under the lee of the Cataloochee Divide. Using only hand tools, he dug a serviceable road between the old Caldwell Fork road and his new home. The road was later improved by the Youth Conservation Corps and afterward christened the Boogerman Trail.

The Boogerman Trail is a loop. It starts from the Caldwell Fork Trail and circles back to the Caldwell Fork Trail, two miles above where it began. On leaving the Caldwell Fork Trail, the Boogerman Trail climbs quickly out of this lush, rhododendron-encumbered valley and onto the drier, northern flank of Den Ridge. Here the forest was spared the woodman's ax, and the poplars, hemlocks, and white pines reach sizes virtually unmatched in any other area of the Park. The area also has one of the highest concentrations of dead chestnuts and chestnut stumps which we have seen in the Park. You can identify them by their bleached-out appearance and the vertical cracks running down their sides.

The trail climbs up Den Ridge for two miles before dropping into an enclosed cove shaded exclusively by tall white pines.

A couple of years ago, we were hiking this stretch when we came upon two young bear cubs wrestling just off the trail. One was a yearling and the other was no more than two or three months old. When they saw us, the little one scurried about seven feet up a tree right in front of us while his big brother ran down the ravine, presumably to go get mommy.

The little cub hung there looking at us for about thirty seconds, getting more nervous all the time. Finally, he could not stand it anymore and quickly backed down the tree, dodged to the next tree, about four feet away, and scurried up to the same seven-foot height, leaving him right where he was to begin with relative to where we were standing. It was at this point that we ran out of courage (came to our senses?) and beat a hasty exit up the trail, not wanting to be confronted by the irate mother. One of the few times that these shy creatures can be dangerous is when a person comes between a sow and her cubs.

After about two miles the trail crosses Palmer Branch on a small footlog and enters a grassy clearing once occupied by Boogerman Palmer's house. In 1929 the Park paid Boogerman a little over five thousand dollars for his homestead and more than 250 acres. The trail continues to the end of the cove and climbs the adjacent ridge to Sag Gap. Shortly after beginning the climb, it passes, on the left, one of the largest poplar trees in the Smokies. Beyond Sag Gap, the trail descends gently into the Snake Branch drainage, shaded by concentrations of chestnut oaks and black gums. Along this stretch, occasional vestiges of pioneer farms, particularly fence posts, stone walls, and building foundations rest in the concealing shadows of the forest. Three hundred yards from its end, the trail passes a small, weedy clearing with the remains of an old barn and log cabin built by Carson Messer.

After a little under four miles the Boogerman Trail rejoins the Caldwell Fork Trail. The Caldwell Fork Trail leads right two miles to the lower Boogerman Trail intersection and left for another two and a half miles until it reaches the pay-off on this hike, Big Poplars. On the way it passes the juncture with the Big Fork Ridge Trail.

In the waning days of the Civil War, Colonel George Kirk, a notorious federal raider who had deserted the Confederacy, rode into Cataloochee with a posse of Union renegades, looting farms and bushwhacking suspected Confederate sympathizers. Kirk and his men entered Caldwell Fork, looking for Levi Shelton and Ellsworth (Elzie) Caldwell, native Cataloochians accused of supporting the Confederacy. The riders followed the ruffled surge of Caldwell Fork through steep-sided ravines flanked by deep entanglements of doghobble and twisted, gnarled rhododendron.

In Kirk's day, the lower Caldwell Fork vicinity was wilderness. There was no graded Boogerman Trail looping up and back to the Caldwell Fork Trail. The first cabin he and his men encountered upstream was probably the Jesse McGee house. Kirk's marauders proceeded further up the mountain to the Caldwell place and whipped the women, hoping to force them into revealing the whereabouts of the men. The women would not tell, so the soldiers waited until night and followed the women when they went to see Levi and Elzie. The soldiers captured the men in their hiding place and took them to be executed at Rabbit Log Gap. Their bodies were covered with chestnut bark and buried in the sinkhole between Rough Fork and Caldwell Fork. Later, their bodies were retrieved and buried again in a single grave on a hillside overlooking the Caldwell Fork Trail.

The trail passes through the center of the cove, intersecting the upper terminus of the Big Fork Ridge Trail and, one hundred yards further, the lower terminus of the McKee Branch Trail. Three hundred yards above the McKee Branch junction, an inconspicuous path runs uphill to the left. At the top of the path is a disused road flanked by a tiny enclosure. It bears the grave of the murdered Levi Shelton and Elzie Caldwell.

Not far above the grave site are the Deadening Fields, so called because of the settler John Caldwell's practice of "deadening" virgin trees by paring off wide strips of bark from around the trunks and waiting for the trees to die. Afterward, Caldwell burned the trees and cleared the area for farming. The Deadening Fields bear few marks of Caldwell's old farm fields; the clearings are now shaded by a sparse copse of uniformly slender pines.

A half-mile beyond the Deadening Fields, the trail intersects the lower terminus of the Hemphill Bald Trail. From this juncture on, the Caldwell Fork Trail is known popularly as the Big Poplar Trail. The Caldwell Fork–Big Poplar Trail climbs briefly, then descends to a footbridge crossing Caldwell Fork. On the far side of the stream are several scattered camping spots known collectively as the Caldwell Fork Backcountry Campsite. One quarter-mile above the Caldwell Fork Camp, a narrow path exits to the right, leading one hundred yards to three poplar trees of staggering proportions standing within a few yards of one another. All three rival the giant poplar in Albright Grove, reputed to be the champion of the Smokies. The three of them together provide a worthy payoff for the energy it takes to get here. The Big Poplars mark the fringe of a rich enclave of virgin forest concentrated along the upper end of Big Fork Ridge.

Retrace your path until you reach the first intersection with Boogerman Trail, where you continue straight down Caldwell Fork Trail. This segment runs two miles until it again passes the lower end of Boogerman Trail. Through here you will make a dozen or so stream crossings, mostly on footlogs. 🚶‍♂️

The Best Short Hikes in the Great Smoky Mountains was designed and typeset on a Macintosh Quadra using PageMaker sotware. The text font is Stone serif, with statistical data set in Stone Sans. The display fonts are Copperplate 33bc and Cochin Bold Italic.

This book was designed by Todd Duren and composed in-house at the press.

The paper used in this book is designed for an effective life of at least three hundred years.